Sir Robert Peel

General Editors: Eric J. Evans and P. D. King

A. L. Beier	The Problem of the Poor in Tudor and Early Stuart England
Martin Blinkhorn	Democracy and Civil War in Spain 1931–39
Martin Blinkhorn	Mussolini and Fascist Italy
Robert M. Bliss	Restoration England 1660–1688
Stephen Constantine	Lloyd George
Stephen Constantine	Social Conditions in Britain 1918–1939
Susan Doran	Elizabeth I and Religion 1558–1603
Christopher Durston	James I
Eric J. Evans	The Great Reform Act of 1832
Eric J. Evans	Political Parties in Britain 1783–1867
Dick Geary	Hitler and Nazism
John Gooch	The Unification of Italy
Alexander Grant	Henry VII
M. J. Heale	The American Revolution
Ruth Henig	The Origins of the First World War
Ruth Henig	The Origins of the Second World War 1933–1939
Ruth Henig	Versailles and After: Europe 1919–1933
P. D. King	Charlemagne
Stephen J. Lee	Peter the Great
Stephen J. Lee	The Thirty Years War
J. M. MacKenzie	The Partition of Africa 1880–1900
Michael Mullett	Calvin
Michael Mullett	The Counter-Reformation
Michael Mullett	James II and English Politics 1678–88
Michael Mullett	Luther
Robert Pearce	Attlee's Labour Governments 1945–51
Gordon Phillips	The Rise of the Labour Party 1893–1931
J. H. Shennan	France Before the Revolution
J. H. Shennan	Louis XIV
David Shotter	Augustus Caesar
David Shotter	Tiberius Caesar
Keith J. Stringer	The Reign of Stephen
John K. Walton	The Second Reform Act
John K. Walton	Disraeli
Michael J. Winstanley	Gladstone and the Liberal Party
Michael J. Winstanley	Ireland and the Land Question 1800–1922
Alan Wood	The Origins of the Russian Revolution 1861–1917
Alan Wood	Stalin and Stalinism
Austin Woolrych	England Without a King 1649–1660

LANCASTER PAMPHLETS

Sir Robert Peel: Statesmanship, Power and Party

Eric J. Evans

London and New York

First published 1991 by Routledge
11 New Fetter Lane,
London EC4P 4EE

Simultaneously published in the USA and Canada
by Routledge
29 West 35th Street, New York, NY 10001

Reprinted 1994

Filmset in Great Britain by
Rowland Phototypesetting Ltd
Bury St Edmunds, Suffolk
and printed in Great Britain by
Clays Ltd, St Ives plc

British Library Cataloguing in Publication Data
Evans, Eric J. (Eric John)
Sir Robert Peel: statesmanship, power and party.
1. Great Britain. Politics, history
I. Title
941.081092

Library of Congress Cataloging in Publication Data
Evans, Eric J.
Sir Robert Peel: statesmanship, power, and party / Eric J. Evans.
p. cm. − (Lancaster pamphlets)
Includes bibliographical references and index.
1. Peel, Robert, Sir, 1788–1850. 2. Prime ministers − Great
Britain − Biography. 3. Great Britain − Politics and
government − 1837–1901. 4 Great Britain − Politics and
government − 1830–1837. I. Title. II. Series.
DA536.P3E84 1991
941.081'092—dc20
[B] 91-10366

ISBN 0-415-06049-4

Contents

Foreword

Lancaster Pamphlets offer concise and up-to-date accounts of major historical topics, primarily for the help of students preparing for Advanced Level examinations, though they should also be of value to those pursuing introductory courses in universities and other institutions of higher education. Without being all-embracing, their aims are to bring some of the central themes or problems confronting students and teachers into sharper focus than the textbook writer can hope to do; to provide the reader with some of the results of recent research which the textbook may not embody; and to stimulate thought about the whole interpretation of the topic under discussion.

Acknowledgements

My indebtedness to all of the scholars who have interpreted and reinterpreted a crowded, fascinating and occasionally confusing period will be evident to anyone familiar with it. However, I have received much specific help from Dr J. A. Carr and my co-editor, Dr P. D. King. Both examined first drafts, offered detailed criticism of my decisions about organization and also made me aware that my familiarity with some of the material was making inappropriate demands on readers coming to it for the first time. Their comments have been invaluable and I am most grateful. Any errors and miscalculations which remain are, of course, my own responsibility.

Many of the ideas offered here have been presented to sixth-form and undergraduate audiences over the past three years. I have benefited enormously from the questions, criticisms and, above all, enthusiasm of student audiences during that time. They have been influential in the final shape of Sir Robert! I hope it is not invidious to acknowledge with great gratitude the stimulus I have received from Patrick Dereham and his pupils at Radley College who provided a congenial, yet critical, atmosphere in which to discuss my ideas. Their enthusiasm persuaded me that it was useful to persevere with Peel. I hope that their judgement will not prove misplaced.

Hornby
November 1990   *EJE*

Chronology

1788   Born at Chamber Hall, Bury, 5 February, the first son and third child of Robert Peel, a wealthy cotton manufacturer.

1800   Goes to Harrow School.

1805   Becomes undergraduate at Christ Church, Oxford, where he had a career of considerable academic distinction.

1809   Thanks to patronage of his father (an MP) and on recommendation of Arthur Wellesley (later Duke of Wellington) becomes MP for the Irish seat of Cashel City, Co. Tipperary, a borough with only twenty-four voters. No contest held.

1810   Becomes Under-Secretary for War and the Colonies in the Tory government of Spencer Perceval, at age of 22.

1812   Becomes Chief Secretary for Ireland in new government of Lord Liverpool.

Becomes MP for another 'rotten' borough, Chippenham (Wilts.).

1814–15 Authorizes firm action to deal with unrest in Ireland – Insurrection and Peace Preservation Acts.

1817   Makes strong speech in Parliament opposing Catholic emancipation. His position on emancipation makes him attractive to Oxford University, whose MP he becomes.

1818   Professing himself 'tired' of the post, he resigns the Chief Secretaryship of Ireland at time of the general election.

1819	Appointed Chairman of the parliamentary committee enquiring into state of finances – the Bullion Committee. His report influential in passage of the Currency Act which provided for transition to resumption of cash payments by Bank of England. Peel's work established his reputation as knowledgeable and effective in economic affairs.
1820	At age of 32 marries Julia Floyd, daughter of a General who had seen service in India and, while Peel was Chief Secretary, Ireland.
1822	Returns to government, and becomes a Cabinet minister for the first time as Home Secretary. Age 34.
1823–4	Gaols Acts rationalize provision of gaols in all towns, and establish system of inspection.
1823	Statutes passed reducing the number of offences which carried the death penalty.
1825	Jury Act rationalizes what had been chaotic practice and makes jury responsibilities and selection procedures much clearer.
1826	Supervises response to outbreaks of industrial unrest especially in Lancashire and Yorkshire. Sends troops to Lancashire and urges magistrates to fair but firm prosecution of offenders.
1826–7	Five Statutes rationalize Criminal Law on theft and other property offences.
1827	Liverpool forced to resign through ill health and Peel refuses to serve in a government headed by Canning, because of Canning's views in favour of Catholic emancipation. Resigns from government.
1828	After death of Canning and failure of subsequent ministry of Goderich, Peel resumes office as Home Secretary and leader of the House of Commons in a new Tory ministry headed by Duke of Wellington.
1829	Supports Roman Catholic emancipation and provokes furious hostility from 'Protestant' Tories. Resigns parliamentary seat at Oxford University over the issue and is beaten by anti-emancipation Tory, Sir Robert Inglis, in subsequent by-election. Returns to Commons for 'pocket' borough of Westbury (Wilts.). Peel's Metropolitan Police Act establishes new professional police commissioners for London.

1830	Forgery Act reduces number of forgery offences for which capital punishment is an applicable penalty. General election and Peel returned for family seat of Tamworth. Revival of parliamentary reform issue puts government on defensive and it resigns after defeat on a technical issue in November. Peel leaves office. His father dies and he inherits the baronetcy as Sir Robert.
1831	Consistently opposes new Whig government proposals for parliamentary reform.
1832	After resignation of Whigs, refuses to serve in a Tory government (May) pledged to reform. Tories lose many seats in first post-reform general election (December). Peel beginning to be recognized as leader of the Tories.
1833	Makes declaration that he would support Whig government when it acted to defend order, law and property.
1834	Stanley and Graham desert Whig government over Irish Church issue. King dismisses Melbourne's government (November) and Peel installed as prime minister in a minority Tory government (December). Issues Tamworth Manifesto, pledging Tories to modest reform.
1835	Ecclesiastical commission established. Tories gain ground at general election, but Peel defeated by new alliance of Whigs and Radicals; returns to opposition.
1836	Works at forging greater unity between Tories in upper and lower Houses of Parliament.
1837	Greater co-operation with Stanley and Graham increases Peel's strength as Conservative leader; further gains in the general election.
1838	Merchant Taylor's Hall speech emphasizes Conservatives' support for preservation of existing institutions in Church and State.
1839	Bedchamber Crisis; Peel refuses to take office when Queen insists on retaining Whig ladies of the Bedchamber.
1840	Disagreements between Peel and Wellington over various issues but Peel persuades Wellington to abandon opposition to Whig Canada legislation. Conservative unity maintained.
1841	Whigs defeated on vote of no confidence (June); this precipitates general election (July) which Conservatives

win. Peel becomes prime minister of a majority government (August).

1842   Budget reintroduces income tax for first time since 1816 and reduces duties on wheat; general reduction of tariffs. The Protectionist Buckingham resigns from Cabinet.

Mines Act prohibits women and children from working underground.

1843   Graham's Factory bill delayed by defeat over educational clauses which would have extended Anglican influence over factory education.

1844   Factory Act reduces hours of work in textile factories. Substantial Tory support for Ashley's motion to secure maximum ten-hour working day. Government defeated but Peel's threat of resignation secures majority for him. Many backbenchers vote against Peel on sugar duties.

Bank Charter Act provides for new currency base by linking Bank of England's power of note-issue to available reserves of bullion.

1845   Gladstone resigns on proposal to increase grant to Irish Roman Catholic seminary at Maynooth; 149 Tories vote against the grant.

Budget renews income tax and introduces substantial reductions of tariff, including abolition of many import duties.

Beginning of Irish potato famine and Peel commits Cabinet to repealing Corn Laws (December). Fails to persuade Russell to take over as prime minister to repeal the Corn Laws.

1846   Bentinck and Disraeli organize Conservative opposition to repeal of Corn Laws (January–February). On vital Corn Law vote, only 112 Tories support Peel and repeal of Corn Laws is carried by Whig/Liberal votes.

Peel defeated on Irish coercion bill (June) and resigns.

Free trade Conservatives act as a separate parliamentary 'Peelite' group, but Peel refuses to act as their party leader.

1847   General election confirms substantial Whig/Liberal majority but about a hundred 'Peelites' refuse to support either main party. Peel offers advice and support to Liberals on free trade policies.

1848   Peel supports Chancellor of Exchequer, Wood, on retention of income tax and increased expenditure on armed forces.

1849   Peelites refuse offer to join Whig/Liberal government. Peel refuses to take any part in negotiations or express any desire to return to office.

Makes speech urging measures to aid economic recovery of Ireland.

Navigation Acts repealed with Peelite support.

1850   Final speech in Parliament (June) criticises Palmerston's foreign policy and urges non-interference in affairs of other nations.

29 June: riding accident and dies on 2 July.

1
Introduction

Sir Robert Peel is, with Gladstone and Disraeli, one of the three most celebrated prime ministers in nineteenth-century British history. In terms of legislative achievement, he was probably the most successful of all. Some argue that his reforms contributed more than those of any other prime minister to improving standards of living for ordinary people. The *Manchester Guardian* referred to a 'most striking and extraordinary expression of popular feeling' on the occasion of Peel's untimely death as the result of a riding accident in July 1850. Those who mourned credited him with giving the poor cheap bread by repealing the Corn Laws in 1846. The often high, and frequently volatile, level of bread prices had been one of the most destabilizing features of early-nineteenth-century Britain, and much misery, leading to economic and social conflict, had resulted. Some historians have also credited Peel with laying the foundations of mid-Victorian prosperity by expert management of national finances and by accelerating freetrade policies which opened up new markets for British manufacturers.

Peel's reputation, therefore, might seem secure. Yet he was a figure of great controversy for much of his lifetime. Recently, also, the extent of his achievements has been reassessed by historians. Those who donated their pennies and their pounds towards Peel Monuments in 1850 probably did not pause to reflect that the man whose memory they were immortalizing in stone had opposed most of the great progressive movements of the age. He had resisted greater civil and political rights for Roman Catholics until fear of a nationalist uprising in Ireland changed his mind in 1829. This *volte face* destroyed Peel's credibility with many of his previously staunchest Tory allies. They never forgave him, and accepted his later leadership of their party with many reservations and profound reluctance. He was not widely trusted within his own party after 1829.

Peel also opposed the passage of the Great Reform Act of 1832. This confirmed him as a main target for hostility at the other end of the politcal spectrum. As with Catholic emancipation, he later accepted the need for reform, but only, as he put it in December 1834, as the 'final settlement of a great Constitutional question'. He resisted further political 'adventures', rejecting both votes for working men and the secret ballot. His opposition to the Chartists' call for democracy in the late 1830s and early 1840s was entirely predictable. At the height of the Chartist disturbances, his effigy was publicly burned in several cities and early in 1843 his private secretary, mistaken for Peel, was assassinated while walking in Whitehall. Predictable also was the fact that, as prime minister, he handled the Chartist threat of 1841–2 with much greater efficiency than his Whig predecessors had done when the movement first gathered mass support in 1838–9.

His one steadfast 'reformist' cause was economic. Believing that they hampered economic growth, and thus the development of national prosperity, Peel consistently supported moves to reduce, and eventually to remove, tariffs, tolls and other encumbrances on trade. He had been an early convert to the ideas advocated so brilliantly by Adam Smith in *The Wealth of Nations*, published in 1776. The logic of these ideas led ultimately to the removal of those tariffs, known as the 'Corn Laws', which protected corn growers and, for much of the first half of the nineteenth century, kept the price of grain high. After Peel's repeal of the Corn Laws in 1846, the Tory party split and the Tories were only rarely in government between 1846 and 1874.

One historian, Boyd Hilton, has recently argued that Peel was imprisoned in free trade ideology and that economic obsessions warped his wider political judgement. Others have praised just this judgement. Lord Blake has seen him as 'pursuing his cautious middle course' and as an exponent of 'consensus politics' while Norman Gash, his most celebrated biographer whose views have won wide acceptance, believed that he looked first not to either party or ideology but 'to the state [and] . . . to national expediency'.

Peel's standing as politician and statesman will be debated later (Chapter 11) but, undoubtedly, his free trade policies led directly to the break-up of the Conservative party over Corn Law repeal. After 1846, the party did not win a majority in Parliament for almost thirty years and had to be content with rare periods of minority government. Tory opponents naturally blamed Peel for destroying the party and for blighting the political careers of a whole generation. The controversy over the Corn Laws throws up an interesting paradox. If, as is widely suggested, Peel deserves the most credit for rebuilding Tory fortunes after the splits and electoral disasters of 1827–32, why was he so apparently determined to pursue a policy which, as he well knew, the majority of his backbenchers would never accept?

Peel's career is fascinating to trace as a narrative, since he was at or near the centre of power for almost forty years during one of the most controversial and formative periods of modern British history. It also throws up some important questions and challenges. Why did a politician with such firm opinions and clarity of mind change that mind on the most crucial questions of the day? Why were these changes so controversial and, eventually, so damaging to his own career? What exactly was the new phenomenon historians have called 'Peelite Conservatism'? How did it differ from the Toryism which had gone before? Did Peel in 1846 destroy his own handiwork by provoking a split in the Conservative party? Is he better seen as an economic ideologue, pursuing free trade against all political reason and judgement, or as a flexible and pragmatic politician? Why was such a controversial and frequently personally unpopular figure so widely venerated as a great national leader so soon after his fall from power? What, ultimately, was his contribution to the development of modern Britain?

The remainder of this Pamphlet tries to provide answers to these questions through an assessment of Peel's varied career. The answers, of course, are not intended to be definitive. Historians must establish facts, so far as they are able, and the great quantity of information available about Peel makes this a relatively easy task. Their main task, however, is to stimulate informed argument and debate about major questions. The importance of Sir Robert Peel is a prime issue on which to focus such a debate.

2
The young statesman, 1809–18

Like almost all successful politicians born in the eighteenth century, Robert Peel came from a wealthy background. Unlike most, however, the Peel family wealth was neither landed in origin nor of long duration. Sir Robert Peel's grandfather had been a small independent farmer in Lancashire. His father, also named Robert, made the family fortune in the infant cotton industry during the early years of the industrial revolution. Peel was, therefore, the first prime minister to come from an industrial background. He was born in Bury in 1788, the first son of the family and, despite expensive education and a lifetime in the company of the great and privileged, never entirely lost his Lancashire accent.

The Peel family showed how easily the very wealthy could move into positions of political influence. Two years after Peel's birth, his father used some of his industrial wealth to buy extensive property in the Tamworth area of Staffordshire, and in 1796 he acquired Drayton Manor, which then became the family's country seat and power base. It was a characteristic of much landed property in the eighteenth century that the right to nominate the local Member of Parliament went with it. Few parliamentary constituencies before 1832 had large electorates and many seats were acknowledged either to be 'part of the estate' or to be available to the highest bidder. Robert senior's purchase enabled him to become one of the two MPs for the borough of Tamworth in 1790. His subsequent parliamentary career was not distinguished. He rarely spoke in the Commons,

4

did not aspire to high office and served, as did so many property owners of his generation, as a loyal supporter of William Pitt the Younger and opponent of the dangerous new doctrines of equality, democracy and 'the rights of man' unleashed by the French Revolution. He is remembered for his part in passing the Health and Morals of Apprentices Act of 1802 and the Factory Act of 1819, the first pieces of legislation which attempted to regulate conditions of factory labour in the new textile industries. He accepted the title of baronet in 1800. His son inherited it on his death in 1830 – hence 'Sir' Robert Peel.

His father's success provided Peel with a magnificent opportunity to follow him into politics. It was clear from early days that young Robert was a highly intelligent boy, with an extremely good memory, a clear mind, formidable powers of organization and lucid exposition. His scholastic career at Harrow and Oxford was distinguished. In 1808, he took a double first-class degree in Classics and Mathematics. Academic distinction, however, was of less importance in getting into the Commons than good connections, and these his father could provide.

Immediately after Robert's graduation, his father put out feelers about possible parliamentary vacancies for him. An opportunity presented itself of an Irish seat with only twenty-four voters where a combination of Peel money and government influence, willingly extended on behalf of a loyal and trusted backbencher, was sufficient to see the young man installed as an MP at the age of 21. By one of those twists of personal irony which often obtain in politics, the necessary arrangements were handled by Arthur Wellesley, later Duke of Wellington. One future Tory prime minister thus smoothed the initial path of another. Relations between Wellington and Peel would be critical to the health of the Tory party for almost twenty years, from the late 1820s to the mid-1840s.

There was nothing unusual about well-connected men getting into parliament in their early twenties. Nor was it surprising that Peel should have been a Tory. Quite apart from his father's convictions, the overwhelming majority of men of property had been thoroughly alarmed by the democratic implications of the French Revolution and saw support for a firm party of order, such as had been fashioned by Pitt the Younger in the years after 1794, as the best guarantee that the contagion of Revolution would not spread to Britain. Peel was easily persuaded of the justice of the Tory cause. Its anti-reformist ideology and the reputation for order and administrative efficiency built up by Pitt suited both Peel's talents and his temperament.

Good connections could not only get a man into parliament early. They could also provide him with opportunities to shine in debate in the Commons. Such opportunities Peel grasped eagerly, and, within a few months of his arrival, he was already being noted on both sides of the House as a 'coming man'. His first ministerial post – Under-Secretary for War and the Colonies in the department headed by Lord Liverpool – was gained as early as 1810. It was not a post which gave much opportunity either for debating fireworks or for independence of expression, but Peel gave Liverpool diligent support during a critical stage of the war with Napoleonic France and discharged the duties of the office with that administrative efficiency which was already becoming a Peelite hallmark. The post proved a useful launching pad for a ministerial career.

Every aspiring politician needs luck as well as ability, and the assassin's bullet which ended the life of the prime minister, Spencer Perceval, in 1812 served to advance Peel's career. After a brief period in which the Prince Regent cast about for more exciting alternatives, Lord Liverpool was appointed as Perceval's successor. He offered the post of Chief Secretary for Ireland to his recent deputy at the war office. Undoubtedly the working relationship which had been established between the two men was a factor in the appointment.

The Chief Secretaryship was not a cabinet post but it was a substantial promotion for a man of 24. It brought Peel to national attention and it presented – as Irish jobs are prone to do for British politicians – a substantial challenge. In Peel's case, the challenge was to reconcile the majority of Irishmen both to the loss of their own parliament in consequence of the Act of Union of 1800 and to government by a Protestant minority under direction from Westminster.

Peel remained Chief Secretary for six years, the longest tenure of the post in the nineteenth century, during which time his resilience and his political skills were fully tested. The function of the Chief Secretary was to represent British government policy in Ireland and to make proposals for action based on direct knowledge of the country. He was not head of the administration in Ireland – the Lord Lieutenant fulfilled that responsibility – but the job was a vital one. It required dual residence – at Westminster during parliamentary sessions and in Dublin for much of the rest of the year. Inadequate roads and frequently choppy or stormy sea crossings combined to make Anglo-Irish travel physically wearing. Peel retained a close interest in Irish matters after he left office in 1818 but it is perhaps not surprising that he never set foot in Ireland again.

Peel's skills were tested, not only by Ireland's problems, but by establishing effective working relations with the permanently-resident Lord Lieutenant. His famous attention to detail, rapid assimilation of a political brief and respect for proper authority combined to make his relationship with the three Viceroys he served generally harmonious. Indeed, Norman Gash noted a 'close personal and political confidence' in the partnership with Viscount Whitworth, Lord Lieutenant from 1813 to 1817, 'which made the Irish administration [in those years] a model of unity and efficiency'.

A number of intricately interwoven political, religious and economic factors made Ireland notoriously difficult for the British to govern. The Union of the two kingdoms had not been accompanied by more political rights for Roman Catholics, and many leading Irish Catholic landowners felt betrayed by a Union they had initially supported as a means of preserving property. Virtually all leading positions in the Irish administration were held by Anglican Protestants, who comprised considerably less than 10 per cent of the population. The 'Protestant Ascendancy' manifested too many instances of complacent corruption in the distribution of offices to inspire confidence, and Peel, a natural Protestant supporter, nevertheless bridled at the provocative distribution of the spoils.

He bridled even more at the aggressive Protestantism, usually of Scottish Presbyterian origin, which was developing among workers in Ulster and viewed the new 'Orange Lodges' with deep suspicion. 'There are many phrases applied to the Association of Orangemen which are of much too military a character to suit my taste', he wrote in 1814. He was, inevitably, a strong supporter of the Union but he feared civil war between the Presbyterian minority and the Catholic majority and was concerned at the narrow power base occupied by an Anglican and aristocratic elite. Efficient though much of his work in Ireland was, it was characterized by a barely suppressed irritation at what he saw as the triviality and petty-mindedness of much of the indigenous population.

This was a typical British reaction. Though he made himself far better informed than most about Ireland, he shared British prejudices about the lawlessness and savagery of the Irish peasantry which from time to time overbore his subtle understanding of the economic basis of their miseries. He feared both the existence of secret

7

societies and the tribal warfare which he believed they provoked. He sought to establish firm authority in Ireland not just because he believed in peace and the rule of law but also because he shared the belief of most of his countrymen that he was dealing with an inferior race at a lower stage of development than the British. The Irish needed firm lessons because they could not understand oblique ones. As an early-nineteenth-century Protestant, also, Peel had a background and upbringing which conditioned him to believe that Roman Catholicism was a primitive, authoritarian religion appropriate only to simple minds and inimical to liberty and freedom of speech.

His prejudices occasionally got the better of his logic. In 1815, he allowed himself to be drawn into a dispute with the Catholic barrister and nationalist leader Daniel O'Connell which almost culminated in a duel at Ostend, where both parties had agreed to meet in order to avoid the authorities. O'Connell it was who first coined the sobriquet 'Orange Peel', not only to describe his opponent's Protestant sympathies as is usually assumed, but also to attack what he called a 'ludicrous enemy . . . a raw youth squeezed out of the workings of I know not what factory in England'.

Religious conflict was the most obvious problem presented by Irish affairs but the economic dimension could never be ignored. Ireland, the linen industry of eastern Ulster apart, was an overwhelmingly rural country. It did not share in the economic advances being made during the first phase of Britain's industrial revolution. What it did share, however, was disturbingly rapid population growth. Between the early 1780s and the early 1820s, the country's population grew from 4 million to almost 7 million, the most rapid growth being concentrated in the remoter western regions of Ireland and the least in the most economically developed north-east. The result was great pressure on landholdings and available foodstuffs and sharply declining living standards for the peasantry. In 1815, Peel proposed to the government a scheme for assisted emigration from Ireland to Canada, but it did not find favour with the prime minister and population pressures continued to mount.

In 1816, the potato crop, on which increasing numbers of Irish folk depended, partially failed and Peel spent much of the first half of 1817 in organizing emergency supplies. About £37,000 was raised for famine relief and substantial movements of food were arranged. The measures were hardly adequate and the government was fortunate that the 1817 harvest was ample enough to see prices fall substantially and take the sharpest edge off the hunger. It was also the case that Peel's policy was motivated as much by fear of widespread violence if nothing were done as by concern for the well-being of the Irish peasant. Nevertheless, his work was widely praised and the famine of 1817 had a happier outcome for Peel and for the Irish than the much more serious potato famine of 1845–6.

Ireland's economic difficulties were compounded by the country's contribution to the protracted war effort against France. By the time the exchequers of Britain and Ireland were united in 1817, the Irish National Debt was 250 per cent higher than it had been at the time of the Union in 1801. Britain contributed much more to the war effort, of course, but its vastly more diverse and expanding economy could better bear the load. During the same period, Britain's debt increased by only 50 per cent. Ireland was suffering from shortages of capital which made the country's post-war economic recovery much more difficult.

Peel's policies as Chief Secretary were dominated not by finance, however, but by problems of order based on the religion. In 1811, Irish Catholics had formed a 'Catholic Board' to co-ordinate activity aimed at achieving greater political rights. Under its umbrella, Daniel O'Connell, leader of what Peel called the 'violent party', orchestrated the single strands of violence into something like a concerted Catholic campaign. This led Peel to recommend the dissolution of the Board in 1814. The dissolution was skilfully timed, against the advice of the Protestant government in Ireland which wanted precipitate action at the height of the crisis, to take effect when internal disunity had already weakened the Catholic cause.

The disturbances of 1812–13 gave Peel the incentive to collect information from across the country about the extent of lawlessness. This evidence he sifted meticulously in order to prepare what became his first substantial legislation. The Peace Preservation Act and the Insurrection Act of 1814 were designed to give greater peace-keeping powers to the authorities by establishing for the first time professional, and salaried, magistrates and full-time local police forces. Appointments, so far as possible, were not to be influenced by established patronage networks, which Peel felt only inflamed Catholic opinion; he looked to old army and militia men to service the new organization. His police policies, of course, foreshadowed the more celebrated initiatives in London fifteen years later. They were also an early instance of using Ireland as a kind of 'social laboratory' in which to try out policies which might have later application on the mainland.

Proposals to allow Catholics to take up government positions and to remove their other legal disabilities came periodically before parliament. Though 'Protestants' (to use the convenient shorthand for those who opposed any form of Catholic emancipation) were advantaged by the absence of consensus on the 'Catholic' side about precisely what rights it was safe to confer, the issue was naturally contentious and provoked damaging disagreements within Liverpool's Tory party. Peel's speech against Henry Grattan's motion for Catholic relief in 1817 proved to be a landmark in his career. Several of his opponents declared it the most able statement of the Protestant case that they had heard; some believed that it swayed a close vote the government's way. It certainly strengthened the government and gave the prime minister further evidence of Peel's potential for high office.

More important perhaps in the light of later developments, it established him on the 'Protestant' wing of the Tory party as an effective champion of their cause. Though Peel resigned his office in 1818, his period as Chief Secretary had important implications for the remainder of his career. He had proved his administrative capability and shown, in the managing of the Protestant administration in Dublin, a high degree of political skill. His policies on law and order in Ireland and against Catholic emancipation, however, conveyed the impression that he was natural leader for the more extreme anti-Catholic Tories in Westminster. In reality, Peel was too ambitious and too shrewd to hitch himself irredeemably to a cause which might well be a political dead-end. Ultimately, however, he was to pay a heavy price for the reputation he acquired as an unswerving Protestant.

3
Peel, the Home Office and 'Liberal Toryism', 1819–30

Peel's reputation depends heavily upon his competence as a finance minister. Yet, until he accepted Liverpool's invitation to chair a parliamentary enquiry into the state of public finances in 1819, he had little economic expertise. Characteristically, however, he was determined to learn, and quickly. The Chairmanship of the Currency Committee gave Peel his first opportunity to play a leading role in British, rather than Irish, politics.

Monetary policy is a technical subject and it is hardly surprising that most MPs did not master it. Its importance, however, was undeniable since government finances were in a frail condition after the return of peace in 1815. Under the weak direction of the Chancellor of the Exchequer, Nicholas Vansittart, government debts mounted. The high interest rates which resulted from the raising of new loans were considered by many of the new breed of 'political economists' to stifle any prospect of post-war economic recovery.

The benefits of tying British currency once again to a fixed standard of value had been advocated cogently by the economist David Ricardo, in *Principles of Political Economy and Taxation* published in 1817. He argued that the supply of credit needed to be reined in and 'sound money' established. His free trade and 'monetarist' ideas, which developed those of Adam Smith, were translated into practical politics by William Huskisson, a junior minister in Liverpool's government. Huskisson was influential in all

11

economic questions but Peel reached his own decision about 'bullion-ism' (as this aspect of Ricardo's ideas was called) and expressed himself intellectually converted to Ricardo's view. British currency had not been linked to a fixed standard of value since Pitt prevented the Bank of England from depleting its reserves by paying its debts and obligations in cash in 1797, during a major financial crisis caused by the wars with Revolutionary France. Peel's committee duly recommended that, after a four-year transitional period, the Bank of England should from 1823 go back on the 'Gold Standard'.

This 'resumption of cash payments' tied to the price of gold was translated into legislation widely known as 'Peel's Act' in 1819. Rural backbench MPs liked the Act because they resented financial manipulations and speculations in the City of London. They did not understand economics but they knew that somewhat dubious for-tunes had been made in the City. Therefore, they wanted its wings clipped and the authority of parliament over financial institutions reasserted. Liverpool, defending 'sound-money' policy in the House of Lords, said that it was necessary to restrain the Bank's 'power of making money, without any check or influence to direct them, than their own notions of profit and interest'. Peel concurred: 'The House [of Commons] had too long transferred its powers [to the Bank and other financial agencies]. Let it recover the authority which it had too long abdicated.'

Political economists believed that leading merchants and manu-facturers had most to gain from Peel's Act but the commercial interests mostly opposed it. Peel's own father presented a petition to the Commons from the merchants of London against any resump-tion of cash payments. Even in Manchester, which later in the century would be acclaimed as both the practical and the intellectual centre of 'sound money', almost 150 leading merchants, bankers and traders wrote an anguished letter to Liverpool. They recognized that they must eventually tread the path of monetary virtue but prayed, St Augustine-like, that it be not yet.

Despite influential opposition, the Bank decided that it did not need the full four-year transition period recommended by Peel's committee. By 1821, Britain was securely back on the Gold Standard. What was to become the dominant financial wisdom of the Victorian age – a sound, metal-based currency buttressed by cheap government, balanced books and, eventually, low rates of direct and indirect taxation – was foreshadowed by the policies followed by Liverpool's government between 1819 and 1822. In putting these policies in place, Robert Peel played an intellectually subordinate but politically substantial role. From 1819 to the end of his life, Peel would be associated with what came to be called 'economic liberalism', a term deriving from the freedom given to industrialists and businessmen to chase markets, increase their profits and thus, at least in theory, improve job prospects for ordinary people and stimulate economic growth for the benefit of all citizens, if not equally. A similar, if simplified, reasoning led Margaret Thatcher to adopt strict 'monetarist policies' in the Conservative governments of the late 1970s and early 1980s. For Peel, as for Thatcher much later, determined political pursuit of an economic theory was to produce strong reactions. If Peel polarized political opinion, as by the mid-1840s he unequivocally did, it was on an economic philosophy grounded in sound money, low taxes and free trade to which he had become an ardent convert in 1819.

Peel was a backbencher during this formative process, having resigned office as Chief Secretary for Ireland in 1818. Newly married and, perhaps more significant, unconvinced of the stability of Liverpool's government during the messy farce of the Queen Caroline divorce scandal, he refused the offer of a Cabinet post as President of the Board of Control when George Canning resigned in December 1820. Almost a year later, however, in calmer political waters, he was offered a more substantial prize – to succeed the tired, ageing and anyway discredited Viscount Sidmouth. Early in 1822, at the age of 34, Peel entered the Cabinet as Home Secretary. During the next five years he was to play a central part in directing Liverpool's government during what is misleadingly called its 'liberal' phase.

'Liberal Toryism' is a phrase which has stuck fast to the period 1822–7. It requires both explanation and apology. It is associated with the broadly reformist policies adopted both in domestic and foreign affairs by ministers generally new to Cabinet rank after a ministerial reshuffle by Liverpool in 1822–3. The new men included Peel at the Home Office, of course, but also Frederick Robinson as Chancellor of the Exchequer, William Huskisson as President of the Board of Trade and George Canning, the most experienced of them, who replaced Viscount Castlereagh as Foreign Secretary when the latter committed suicide in August 1822. Each of these ministers introduced policies which, at first sight, seem to be turning points. Huskisson, in particular, and Robinson reduced both tariffs and the number of trading monopolies, and also lowered taxes. Canning gave cautious support to nationalism abroad. Britain seemed to become the champion of nations 'struggling to be free' from old, imperialist powers – the Greeks from the Ottoman Turks in southern Europe, for example, and Brazil and Buenos Aires from Portugal and Spain in South America. Peel's reforms are discussed below.

Liberal Toryism has seemed an appropriate term partly because a younger generation replaced the older one represented by Sidmouth, Vansittart and Castlereagh. It also offers a contrast with the less libertarian policies which the Liverpool government adopted during the economic and political difficulties of 1815–20. During these years unemployment was widespread, prices were high and 'hunger politics' stimulated greater support for radical politics. They witnessed the 'Peterloo Massacre' (1819), which occurred when a political meeting calling for parliamentary reform was forcibly broken up by the local yeomanry, and the 'Cato Street Conspiracy' (1820), an attempt by an extreme radical group to blow up members of the Cabinet.

In fact, as I have explained more fully elsewhere (*Britain before the Reform Act*, see Select bibliography, p. 79), Liverpool's government did not experience anything so unsettling as a political or ideological conversion in the early 1820s. Rather it reacted to changing circumstances, perceiving much greater danger to the social fabric in the political activities of the later 1810s than it did in the more buoyant and generally prosperous climate of the 1820s. In many respects, the 'new' policies of the 'liberal Tories' were a continuation and an acceleration of those begun by William Pitt the Younger in the 1780s, before the French Revolution polarized Europe and dominated the thinking of an entire generation.

In the early 1990s, we describe some statesmen of the 1940s, 1950s and 1960s as 'cold-war warriors' when we seek to describe the climate of conflict which sharply divided East and West into the armed camps of communism and capitalism after the end of the Second World War. The French Revolution had a similarly profound effect on the generations of Liverpool and Peel. They sincerely believed that they were fighting to support the old order, hereditary privilege and civilized values against what that quintessentially anti-French Revolutionary warrior Edmund Burke called 'rash and speculative opinion' which threatened to destroy the world they knew. Liberal Toryism in the 1820s should perhaps more appropriately be seen as the first, cautious recognition that the old world had not been destroyed and that governments could safely adapt to

14

change rather than manning increasingly anachronistic ideological barricades. As we shall see, however, 'liberal Toryism' had a predominantly economic and administrative focus. It did not extend to embracing parliamentary reform, while the religious question was a deeply divisive issue within the party.

Nowhere in the final phase of Liverpool's government is the emphasis on continuity rather than change between the 1780s and the 1820s more apt than in the stewardship of the Home Office by Robert Peel. Like Pitt, Peel was more effective as an administrator and codifier than as an innovator, and the Home Office presented a peculiarly appropriate challenge. He is remembered for his work in four fields: law, prisons, trade unions and police.

In the first two of these, which were also the most administratively complex, rationalization was the overriding requirement. The argument for change had already been effectively deployed, particularly by the prison reformer John Howard and by the Whig politicians and intellectuals Samuel Romilly, Thomas Folwell Buxton and Sir James Mackintosh. Similarly, the case for a professional police force which would deter crime as well as prosecute wrongdoers had been advanced by Henry and John Fielding in the middle of the eighteenth century and by the impressive Scottish lawyer and statistician Patrick Colquhoun at the end. On trade unions, Peel was responding to initiatives and, as he saw them, to the important errors made by Francis Place and the Edinburgh surgeon turned radical MP Joseph Hume. Like Pitt, Peel, having been intellectually convinced by the arguments of others, used his formidable organizational powers to bring about necessary change.

English law by the 1820s was chaotic. Over the centuries, new statutes had been introduced to meet a wide variety of circumstances and the legal system had become increasingly complex and confusing. Over two hundred offences, many of them trivial, carried the death penalty at the judge's discretion. In consequence, juries, well aware of the possible consequences, refused to convict felons for fear of condemning them to strangulation on the gallows. After 1815 it seemed that the country was suffering an increasing crime rate and Peel was concerned that the law lacked popular respect because of its theoretical, but in practice capriciously selective, savagery.

In 1823 he passed five statutes greatly reducing the number of capital offences. The opening up of Australia after 1788 provided a convenient repository to house Britain's 'undesirables'. Juries would convict more readily when the likely punishment was transportation rather than death. Transportation was also an eligible solution to the problem of overpopulation. Not until 1801 did British politicians have a reliable indication of the country's population and not until 1811 could they work out how rapidly it was growing.

Peel's Jury Act of 1825 rationalized the rules governing jury selection. In 1826 and 1827, determined, as he put it, to 'break the sleep of a century', he introduced two famous consolidating statutes. The first aimed at improving the administration of central justice. The second removed ninety-two pieces of legislation concerned with theft and other offences against property. Five much clearer and more workable statutes were substituted 'to accommodate the laws relating to crime to the present circumstances and the improved state of society'. These new statutes covered more than 80 per cent of the most common offences. In 1830, during Wellington's government, Peel completed his legal reforms with a statute reducing the number of forgery offences which carried the death penalty.

Peel's approach to prison reform was likewise functional. In 1823, the Gaols Act made possible for the first time a national policy on prisons. Each county and large town was now required to maintain its own gaol or house of correction, funded by local rates. Eighteenth-century gaols, numerous but often unstructured and unsupervised, now came within a standard system of discipline. Inspection by local Justices of the Peace was also introduced. An amending Act in 1824 provided a code for the classification and, if necessary, physical separation of different categories of prisoner. As with legal reforms, Peel followed the lead of others, but he showed sound judgement in selecting workable from fanciful, or wildly expensive, solutions.

Peel's direct involvement with trade union legislation derived from the problems attending the legalization of unions (or 'combinations' as they were called) by the Combination Act of 1824. Trade unions had been formally prohibited by an Act passed by Pitt's government in 1799. The campaign to lift this ban, always a priority for radical leaders among working men, had been taken up by an increasingly influential group of political economists who were followers of Jeremy Bentham. Benthamites like J. R. McCulloch used the existing climate of liberality in economic matters to argue that government legislation should not be used to stop men from working together to raise wages and protect their jobs. Evidence was mounting, especially from the north-east and from Staffordshire, that mine owners were exploiting the artificial weakness of workers which the Combination Acts ensured. In this climate, and with adroit political lobbying organized by Francis Place and Joseph Hume in 1824, it was possible to persuade a more than half-empty House of Commons to repeal these Acts.

Repeal during a climate of economic expansion, however, encouraged an immediate rash of strikes in the cotton, coal and shipbuilding industries. These strikes led to attacks on strikebreakers and alarmed the authorities. Peel and William Huskisson worked together to produce an amending Act in 1825. This preserved the legality of trade unions but introduced fresh penalties for those who made threats or used undue persuasion on workers either to join a union or to go on strike. As Peel explained: 'Men who . . . have no property except their manual skills and strength, ought to be allowed to confer together . . . for the purpose of determining at what rate they will sell their property. But the possession of such a privilege justifies, while it renders more necessary, the severe punishment of any attempt to control the free will of others.'

Peel first took an interest in policing during his years as Chief Secretary for Ireland, when he helped to create a Police Preservation Force there. He did not, however, envisage the creation of a unified, professional and preventive police force for the whole of England while Home Secretary. He was sensitive to the long tradition of English localism, whereby law and order was considered a problem best solved by the co-operation of property owners at parish and county level. Backbench MPs representing the English counties took much persuading that any government intervention in police matters was justified, and the notion of a central agency with responsibility for prosecuting offenders was anathema, smacking of inquisitions and improper interference.

Peel proceeded slowly and obliquely, first establishing parliamentary committees of enquiry to consider the need for policing. His attention was anyway focused on the peculiar problems of London, a city with a population ten times larger than any other in Britain whose public order problems were widely considered unique. As the capital, of course, its difficulties were more apparent to men of influence who lived there for part of the year. Peel used the Home Office's direct control over the Bow Street force, near Covent Garden in the West End, to expand its numbers in 1822. He appointed twenty-four uniformed officers who conspicuously patrolled central London by day to deter crime.

Not until Peel's second stint at the Home Office, in Wellington's government of 1828–30, was a more permanent solution found. The Metropolitan Police Act of 1829 established Britain's first professional, preventive police force. The capital – the small and already well-policed City of London apart – was divided into five sections under the control of two police commissioners, responsible directly to Peel. The force was initially established at three thousand men, many of these recruited from existing 'Bow Street Runners' and also from ex-members of the Army. Initial recruitment was easy but there was a rapid turnover and only during the 1830s, during the competent leadership of the first two commissioners, Charles Rowan (an army veteran both of the Peninsular War and of the Battle of Waterloo) and Richard Mayne (the son of an Irish judge and a lawyer himself, practising in England), was continuity and efficiency established. The basis of police organization inaugurated in London was adopted by other forces as they emerged under later legislation passed by Whig and Liberal governments in 1839 and 1856.

Peel's time as Home Secretary consolidated a reputation first established in Ireland. When illness forced Liverpool to resign early in 1827, Peel was not yet 40, but he was known throughout Westminster as a highly competent minister. His statements to the Commons now carried a practised authority. He did not speak there without being sure of his ground. Not a naturally gifted orator, he nevertheless rarely spoke less than soundly and, at his best, he crushed opponents with the accumulated weight of unchallengeable information.

Despite, or perhaps because of, these gifts, however, he was much more admired than loved. Contemporaries detected a frostiness, aloofness, even arrogance, underlying that massive competence. His concern for administrative detail did not obscure the nature of his Toryism. He was known to support policies which buttressed the positions of the leading 'economic' ministers, Robinson and Huskisson. On a less cerebral plane, and on matters more obviously divisive within the Tory party, he was a known opponent of further measures of Catholic relief, either in Ireland or Britain. So important was the religious question that this position alone placed him on the right of the Tory party in the company of ministers like Eldon, an adamantine reactionary, and Wellington. On the left, favouring Catholic emancipation, stood Canning, who saw himself as Liverpool's natural successor, and Peel's economic ally, William Huskisson.

Even before Liverpool departed the scene, political divisions over religion were becoming worrying for the Tories. From 1827 onwards, they blew them apart and in doing so fashioned a new role for Robert Peel.

4

The collapse of the old Tory party, 1827–32

Lord Liverpool suffered a stroke in February 1827. It left him partially paralysed and necessitated his resignation a few weeks later. His departure severely exacerbated divisions in the party over which he had presided for almost fifteen years. The King confirmed Canning in his expectation that he should succeed Liverpool as prime minister, but the Tory 'right' was reluctant to back such a firm supporter of Catholic emancipation. Peel's opposition to Canning turned exclusively on the Catholic question. Peel was as opposed as ever to 'carrying the Catholic question' and thus 'of injuring the Protestant Constitution of the country'.

As Peel well knew, however, personal factors also came into it. Few of Canning's cabinet colleagues had escaped his famously lacerating tongue and it was no surprise when about forty of those who had held office under Liverpool resigned. They included Wellington, Peel, Eldon, Westmorland and Bathurst from the previous Cabinet. Among their replacements, Canning included three Whig supporters, Lansdowne, Tierney and Carlisle, so that what had seemed since the early years of the nineteenth century to be a clear division in parliament between Whigs and Tories now became much more complex.

Canning's government, though it lasted only a few months because the new prime minister died suddenly in August 1827, was significant in that it involved the loosening of party ties. His replacement, Viscount Goderich, proved as ineffective a leader as he had been a competent subordinate (as Frederick Robinson) under Liverpool. He preserved the new political balance for only a few months before, unable to resolve growing cabinet dissension, he tearfully tendered his resignation to George IV in the first few days of 1828.

The King almost immediately sent for the Duke of Wellington to form a ministry. Wellington recognized Peel's importance and asked him to resume office as Home Secretary. Peel had high hopes of Wellington's ministry. He wrote to his wife: 'My view is to reunite the old Party which was in existence when Lord Liverpool's calamity befell him.' For a few months, these hopes seemed realistic. The Canningite followers, led by Huskisson, came back into the ministry and the few Whigs who had served Canning and Goderich refused to remain in a ministry led by such a firm anti-reformist Tory as Wellington. Thus, the old allegiances seemed secure again. Since the new ministry would survive for almost three years, moreover, it might be concluded that an appropriate degree of stability had been re-established.

In reality, the Wellington ministry proved disastrous for the fortunes of the Tory party. Wellington's soldierly background had trained him to think in terms of black and white and, though he was not totally lacking in political ability, he lacked both the subtlety and the flexibility required to heal Tory wounds. He never quite understood why political subordinates in Cabinet and party were not amenable to obeying orders honestly given in the interests of King and Country, as their military counterparts were.

Disagreements within the Cabinet over the decision finally to remove most of the remaining disabilities from Protestant dissenters by repealing the seventeenth-century Test and Corporations Acts and over Huskisson's plan to introduce a modest reform of the Corn Laws in the spring of 1828 did not bode well. Personal animosities, as so often in politics, were sharpened on what might otherwise have been trivial disagreements and it was no real surprise when Huskisson resigned on one such minor matter – the redistribution of a parliamentary constituency – in May 1828. His supporters followed him out of office and, despite Peel's hopes, by the end of the spring the basis of support for Wellington's administration was worryingly slanted towards the 'Ultra', pro-Protestant, wing. It was the very situation Peel had hoped to avoid.

Neither Peel nor Wellington were bigoted defenders of the Church of England. The failure of a broadly based Tory party to re-establish itself in 1828, however, led Ultras unwisely to believe that both would preserve the Protestant Constitution, as established after the Glorious Revolution of 1688, against any assault. For the Ultras, to give votes to Catholics was to subvert the constitution. Peel's record as Chief Secretary for Ireland was sufficient indication that the Home Secretary was indeed 'Orange Peel' and could be trusted to stand firm against growing calls for Catholic emancipation. They forgot that he had supported bills to give votes to English Catholics in 1823 and 1824, and they overlooked his substantial contribution in Commons debates to securing the repeal of the Test and Corporations Acts, which many Ultras considered the thin end of a wedge of capitulation to the Catholics.

A further problem was the Ultras' justifiable belief that public opinion was on their side. In so far as the most recent general election – that in 1826 – had been indicative of anything, it had been that candidates who opposed giving votes and other liberties to Catholics did well. Parliamentary opinion as a whole had moved more substantially in the direction of giving appropriate political liberties to Protestant dissenters and to Catholics than public opinion had. Parallels exist here with the situation in our own day when support for capital punishment is much higher outside than within parliament.

The religious question by the end of 1828, therefore, had substantially weakened Tory unity. Events in 1829 would destroy it and, as part of this process, have permanent consequences for Peel's political career. Growing parliamentary liberality would almost certainly have extended from Protestant dissenters to Catholics had the question been restricted to Britain. Catholics in England, much of Scotland, and Wales were still a relatively small minority and offered little threat. The 'Catholic question', however, was essentially an Irish one. More than three-quarters of Irish people were Catholics and, under the leadership of Daniel O'Connell, they had become much better organized in the 1820s through the Catholic Association. Those who opposed Catholic emancipation in the late 1820s, therefore, were not just concerned about the supremacy of the Church of England, important though this remained to the Ultras. They feared emancipation as a stalking horse for nationalism and the repeal of the recent Act of Union between Britain and Ireland. This, in its turn, would risk the integrity of the British Empire.

By one of those ironies which give spice to political life, the resignation of the Huskissonites from Wellington's government precipitated the Tory crisis over Catholic emancipation. The President of the Board of Trade had resigned to be replaced by an Irish MP, William Vesey Fitzgerald. By the political rules of the age, his acceptance of a government post required him to submit himself to re-election. Knowing Wellington's government to be less well disposed towards Catholic emancipation than Canning's, the Catholic Association had recently been agitating with particular vigour. It was now ready for a well-publicized test of its strength and Fitzgerald was opposed by O'Connell himself, who duly won the by-election. Since, under the law as it stood in 1828, the Catholic O'Connell was permitted to stand for election but not to take his seat if elected, this event brought the Catholic issue to the forefront of British politics.

Wellington could make calculations about the need to provide Catholic emancipation in Ireland on quasi-military criteria. Forces in favour were: the overwhelming majority of the Irish population; an Irish Chief Secretary who by the autumn of 1828 was seriously alarmed about the extent of civil disorder and the prospect of rebellion; a House of Commons in which a substantial majority for emancipation existed; the inadvisability of dissolving parliament and calling fresh elections. In a few large constituencies, public opinion would ensure the return of an extra 'Protestant' or two but an election would divide the Tories still further and produce no significant redistribution in the balance of forces on the Catholic question. Forces against amounted to only two: a 'Protestant' King who would certainly be difficult and had already made his views clear; and a substantial minority of Protestant Ultras in the Commons who would feel betrayed. No general would fight for the purity of the Protestant constitution on such a battlefield with any expectation of success and Wellington, if a limited politician, was a good general.

Peel had reached a similar conclusion, but his personal position was more vulnerable. His 'Protestant' credentials had been firmly established, at least in the eyes of the Ultras, during his time in Ireland. He had been invited to represent Oxford University as an MP largely on this reputation. Peel had hoped to avoid having to support Catholic emancipation as a minister, knowing the consequences it would have for his credibility among many Tories. However, the deteriorating situation in Ireland, the patent inability of the Marquis of Anglesey, the Lord Lieutenant, and Peel's sense of loyalty to Wellington all contributed to the fateful decision, made at the beginning of 1829, to help frame a Catholic Emancipation Bill.

The Bill, which Parliament first saw in March 1829, and which was law by mid-April, owed much to Peel's administrative brain. It also reflected the objective to which he was groping as a solution to the Irish dilemma and to which he would return as prime minister in the early 1840s: cementing the Union by securing the loyalty to it of the wealthier Catholic gentry and middle-class families. Thus, by the Emancipation Act, Catholics were permitted to hold virtually all offices of State except a few in the King's household, but the qualification to vote in Irish county seats was raised from the old 40s (£2) freehold to £10. This would keep out ill-educated, and quite possibly priest-controlled, Catholic peasants, while enfranchising all those with adequate property.

There was no chance that emancipation would 'solve' the Irish question in the long term, but it was a sufficient concession to O'Connell to stave off the immediate threat of civil war. As Peel had anticipated, however, emancipation destroyed his reputation with the Protestant party not only in Ireland and among backbench MPs but also in the industrial Lancashire from which he had sprung and which was now experiencing increasing waves of Irish immigration. Peel was branded an apostate; neither his decision to resign his Oxford University seat and seek re-nomination nor a careful explanation of his new views in the Commons was of much help. He was defeated in Oxford and had quickly to find a new seat. To the Commons he said 'I yield . . . to a moral necessity which I cannot control, unwilling to push resistance to a point which might endanger the Establishments that I wish to defend'. The speech made a favourable short-term impression, but did not assuage the longer-term wrath of the Protestants. As Norman Gash puts it, Peel had been 'the idolized champion of the Protestant party; that party now regarded him as an outcast'. His 'betrayal' in 1829 was neither forgiven nor forgotten. As we shall see, it was to prove a formidable obstacle in the way of Peel's aim in the 1830s and 1840s to build a new 'Conservative' party from the rubble of that Toryism which collapsed between 1827 and 1832.

It is tempting in a secular age to brand the Ultras as ignorant bigots. Some no doubt were, but the Ultra case is not so lightly dismissed and at crucial points in the remainder of his career, Peel suffered for discounting their arguments. Peel was extremely able, but he was also proud, could be arrogant and found empathy with those of contrary views extremely difficult. A fatal flaw in his character was that, once convinced himself of the validity of an argument, he tended to regard it as proven and those who were not convinced as either mischievous or intellectually inferior.

In 1829, the Protestant party could deploy the respectable argument that legal privileges for the Church of England were an essential prop of the old Constitution which, as they bitterly reminded Peel and Wellington, was a constitution in Church *and* State. As the history of the sixteenth and seventeenth centuries had taught them, Catholicism was equated with tyrannical kings and the threat of foreign rule. Peel, they argued, might have bought temporary peace in Ireland, but he had destroyed the Constitution he had been brought up to respect and defend. For a Tory in the late 1820s, no charge was more serious.

Wellington's government survived the immediate anger and frustration of the Ultras, and Peel, immediately after the conclusion of his contentious labours on emancipation, introduced Metropolitan police legislation (see Chapter 3). There was no denying, however, that the government had been severely damaged by the resolution of the Catholic question. The onset of economic depression and the related revival of the parliamentary reform question in 1829–30 presented challenges which, ultimately, it could not resist. That story has been told in another pamphlet (*The Great Reform Act of 1832*, see Select bibliography, p. 80). Suffice it to say here that a combination of personal rivalries and the divisive nature of the religious question had shattered Liverpool's Tory party and left it ill-equipped to respond to these new challenges.

Any opportunity, never particularly strong, of broadening the base of the administration to include more reformist Tories was lost because of Wellington's confident rejection of the need for parliamentary reform. The government lost some prominent supporters in the election of June 1830, necessitated by the death of George IV. It eventually fell in November, to be replaced by a Whig government headed by Earl Grey and pledged to bring in parliamentary reform.

It is doubtful if Peel regarded loss of office as anything other than a burden relieved. His work as Home Secretary, and increasingly as first lieutenant to Wellington, had been punishing and not very rewarding. He took on extra-departmental duties and chafed at correcting what he saw as the blunders and omissions of others. His political integrity had been seriously challenged for the first time over Catholic emancipation and his reputation dented. Peel was never close to Wellington personally, and he was actively disliked in his social circle. Personal tragedy, in the shape of his father's death in

May 1830, also depressed him. He inherited the baronetcy (and was henceforth Sir Robert), had ample wealth and enjoyed a stable and successful marriage. It was no convenient euphemism for Peel to say at the end of 1830 that he looked forward to spending more time with his family; it was a simple truth.

But it was rest and recuperation Peel craved, not permanent retirement. In November 1830 he was 42 years old and he knew perfectly well, especially after the death of Huskisson at the opening of the Liverpool–Manchester railway two months earlier, that he was the natural successor to Wellington. His ambitions certainly encompassed being prime minister, but over what political configuration he might preside was uncertain. The rapidly changing shape of party politics, soon to be affected once more by the Reform Act, needed digestion. Though Peel was established as a leader, it was not clear who would follow him and on what terms.

Peel was to remain out of office for almost exactly four years, but there was one occasion on which his return seemed likely. The Whigs found passing parliamentary reform a gruelling and thankless task. In May 1832, faced by apparently intractable opposition from William IV over creating fifty new Whig peers to ensure that the bill passed the Lords, Grey tendered his resignation and the King asked Wellington to form a government. The so-called 'Days of May' were a time of high excitement and much agitation during which many contemporaries believed, and some historians have agreed, that a revolution was possible. Peel's position on reform had been explained to the House of Commons. He refused to condemn the principle of reform outright, but made it very clear that the Whigs' bill went too far, threatening the eventual transfer of sovereignty from parliament to the people. In a famous phrase he explained that he was also 'unwilling to open a door which I saw no prospect of being able to close'.

In May 1832, however, he refused to join a Tory government whose sole purpose would be to pass an acceptable reform bill and it is generally accepted that Peel's refusal scuppered Wellington's chances, leaving the King with no choice but to accept the Whigs back on their own terms. Peel was accused of deserting Wellington and also, indirectly, of reducing royal authority – a serious charge against a Tory politician. He could reply that, thinking reform inevitable, it was better passed by the Whigs who had originally sponsored it, and that for the Tories suddenly to take up the issue would be to sacrifice consistency and risk losing public respect.

Without much doubt, however, the real reason for Peel's refusal was the political consideration that his career could not stand a second *volte face* on an issue of principle. He had recanted on Catholic emancipation in 1829; he could not risk Tory fury a second time.

The Tories were condemned to pay a high electoral price for their opposition to parliamentary reform. In the first election for the reformed parliament, held in December 1832, Tory strength in the Commons was reduced to 175 seats at most. Peel was now, by default and by general assumption, the Tories' leader but they were a bedraggled and demoralized group, not at all like the confident party of order over which Liverpool had presided during Peel's long political apprenticeship. Peel in 1832 needed not just to lift morale but to find organizing principles and ideas around which a Tory revival could be mounted.

5

A King's minister out of office: Peel in the 1830s

During the nine years immediately after the passing of the Great Reform Act, the Whigs were in office almost without a break. First Earl Grey and then Viscount Melbourne headed administrations responsible for important measures which many historians have seen as justifying the title sometimes given to the 1830s: 'the decade of reform'.

A new and more rational system of governing Britain's cities and larger towns was made possible by the passage of the Municipal Corporations Act of 1835. The annual elections for town councillors would soon prove an important means of heightening political awareness in early Victorian England. In 1834, a new, and highly controversial, poor law was enacted which saved money but created much antagonism in the towns of midland and northern England, whose problems it had not been passed to solve. An important series of measures to reform the Church of England followed between 1836 and 1840, and a State system for the registration of births, marriages and deaths was introduced in 1837. Also in these years, parliament abolished slavery in the British Empire, passed the first factory legislation buttressed by government inspection, and voted the first State grant in aid of education for the lower classes.

Most of these reforms were a response to the rapid and radical changes being brought about by industrial revolution. The calamitous events of 1827–32 had seen the Tory party branded as the party which opposed reform – in some cases even into the last ditch. The

Whig reforms of the 1830s, therefore, seemed in tune with the mood of the nation and it might be thought that a thoroughly demoralized Tory party could only look resentfully on.

The truth is not so straightforward. Ferocious opponents of all change there certainly were among the Tories, but the party's leading spokesmen were not among them. Indeed, Peel, now recognized on all sides as the leading Tory spokesman in the lower House, went out of his way in responding to the King's speech at the opening of Parliament in January 1833 to deny that he was an anti-reformer: 'He was for reforming every institution that really required reform; but he was for doing it gradually, dispassionately, and deliberately in order that the reform might be lasting'. Peel did not speak as leader of the opposition – a post as yet unknown to the Constitution. Rather he was making an early declaration to the newly elected parliament of his open-mindedness on the leading questions of the day. It was not a speech to win over his Ultra opponents but it was designed to indicate to all who looked to Peel for leadership that the party of Pitt and Liverpool must adapt to survive.

Peel was playing for high stakes. He knew that steadfast opposition to all reform was a sure route to political oblivion but he also held a deeply conservative view of the Constitution. He retained a profound belief in the importance of keeping executive government in the hands of an elite with the background, education and expertise to discharge their responsibilities efficiently and in the national interest. He feared that the crisis over reform had given public opinion too great an influence in the affairs of the nation and he was anxious to reassert executive supremacy over extra-parliamentary influence. Like most political figures of his age, Peel was undemocratic. He believed that 'the people' lacked the education and the judgement to take important decisions. If the nation's legislators acted under pressure from outside, the quality of their judgement would be impaired and national well-being threatened.

The distinction between government by the people and government in the interests of the people was crucial, and Peel expressed it neatly during a debate on the reform bill in 1831: 'We are here to consult the interests of the people, and not to obey the will of the people.' This issue was far more important than party disagreements between Whigs and Tories, political groupings overwhelmingly of the privileged, and heavily dependent on hereditary wealth. Peel's overriding commitment was to good government, discharged by men of responsibility and efficiency. The representative basis of that government was a secondary consideration.

Peel's political objectives in the 1830s were threefold: first, to strengthen government and put 'public opinion' in its place; second, to ensure, so far as was possible since he was out of office, that necessary changes strengthened, rather than weakened, both the Constitution and Britain's governing elite; third, to dispel the image of the Tory party as one of narrow reaction supported only by a small, unrepresentative proportion of the population. The third of these objectives meant taking on, and beating, the Ultras. As is evident, this agenda is one which sits uneasily with modern conceptions about the role of the leader of the opposition, whose primary purpose is to provide 'loyal opposition' to the measures proposed by the government of the day.

Peel in the 1830s was not a leader of the opposition in this sense. For the first few years he was not even the official leader of the Tories. Various overtures were made for a reconciliation between himself and the Ultras. Before 1834, they foundered on mutual distrust and lack of sympathy. In essence, the Ultras feared that Peel would 'rat' again, as he had done in 1829. While Peel did not trust the Ultras to behave responsibly he also denied their qualification for political influence, believing rather too uncritically the stereotype of the 'hunting, shooting and fishing' squire whose politics were dictated purely by considerations of the self-interest of English landowners.

Peel became the unequivocal leader of his party only at the end of 1834. In February of that year, relations between Peel and the Ultras still cool, the diarist Charles Greville was even envying Peel's position as a man of wealth, ability and leisure 'unshackled by party connections and prejudices'. The change in this position came unexpectedly when, in November 1834, King William IV dismissed the Whig ministry of Melbourne and asked the Tories to form an administration. The King's original invitation went to the Duke of Wellington, and it was the old soldier's assertion that prime ministers should now carry authority in the Commons which ensured that the King's commission was transferred to Peel. Peel hurried back from an enjoyable autumn holiday in Italy with his wife and daughter and on 10 December accepted from the King the post of First Lord of the Treasury – which, until the mid-twentieth century, remained the senior official title of the prime minister.

Peel could argue, therefore, that his authority as leader of the

Tories was a by-product of appointment by the King to the most senior government office. If the Tories supported Peel in parliament, then he was *de facto* their leader. He did not become prime minister because he was leader of a party in the Commons. This may seem a precious constitutional distinction but it was central to Peel's perception of the role of a minister. That perception did not change between then and the end of his career. He saw himself as an executive servant of the King first – very much on the model of eighteenth-century prime ministers – and the leader of a party second. The distinction would prove crucial during the great crisis of the Conservative party over the repeal of the Corn Laws in 1845–6 (see Chapter 10).

Despite the consensus among historians, only recently challenged by Ian Newbould, that the 1830s were a decade not only of reform but also of increasingly clear party division between Whigs and Tories, some important caveats must be made. First, although voting records in the Commons suggest that most MPs now voted consistently according to the wishes of their political leaders, a substantial number did not and some, though a dwindling number, continued to reject party labels. Britain in the 1830s did not have a 'two-party system' in the modern sense.

Second, the powers of the monarchy, though likewise dwindling, had not evaporated. Peel became prime minister in 1834 only because William IV dismissed his previous government. It proved to be the last occasion on which a monarch would get rid of a government with a workable majority in Parliament, but contemporaries could not know this. The monarch in the 1830s was more than the titular head of State and the phrase 'the King's minister' was not an empty one. Peel resigned after his brief 'Hundred Days' Ministry in April 1835 not because he had just suffered a damaging defeat in the Commons but because he felt that, without a majority there, he could not guarantee to pass necessary measures. Not to do so would weaken the executive. Similarly, when Queen Victoria offered him the prime ministership again in 1839 he refused it, during the so-called 'Bedchamber Crisis', not because of weakness in the Commons (where his position was considerably stronger than it had been in 1834) but because the Queen would not dismiss ladies of the bedchamber appointed under the previous Whig government. Peel interpreted the new Queen's loyalty to well-liked court appointees as a sign of lack of trust in him and would not take office without an overt sign of the Queen's support.

The third, and perhaps most important, reason for doubting that the 1830s was a decade of two-party politics in the modern sense concerns the nature of the opposition that Peel mounted. Both major parties, then as now, were fairly loose coalitions of interests. However, Peel was concerned that the Whigs had become associated with groups who, though they generally supported Whig ministers in Parliament, did not support their, or Peel's, overall philosophy of government. Historians usually term these groups 'the Radicals', and sometimes talk of the Whig–Radical party in the 1830s. No such party existed. The so-called 'Radicals' comprised a heterogenous group of politicians who fostered a wide range of political causes, including nationalism or separatism in Ireland and further political reform. Some were out-and-out democrats. What they tended to have in common, apart from a belief that the Whigs were a softer touch on reform than the Tories, was a belief in the importance of extra-parliamentary pressure and agitation to achieve their objectives.

It was this, of course, which so alarmed Peel and, to a large degree, shaped the nature of his opposition in the 1830s. It was far more important to him to defeat a radical challenge based on outside pressure than it was to beat the Whigs. Defeating the Radicals often meant supporting the Whigs, and the idea of allying with Radicals in order to bring down the government was utterly unacceptable, much to the chagrin of more 'party-minded' Tories. Peel's underlying strategy was explained to his friend Goulburn, in letters written in 1833 and 1834: 'Our policy ought to be rather to conciliate the goodwill of the sober-minded and well-disposed portion of the community, and thus lay the foundation of future strength.' 'My opinion is decidedly against all manoeuvring, and coquetting with the Radicals, for the mere purpose of a temporary triumph over the Government. . . . If it [the government] breaks up . . . in consequence of a union between Radicals and Conservatives, in my opinion the Government which succeeds it will have a very short-lived triumph.'

Peel's 'opposition', therefore, involved sustaining the government when it passed measures which he considered to be in the national interest and, especially, when it stood firm against one or other of the radical pretensions. In the parliamentary session of 1833, admittedly one during which Peel was not officially the Tory leader and when 'sound government' immediately after the passage of the Reform Act was especially necessary, he voted against the Whigs in only three out of forty-three parliamentary divisions. On the biggest questions, such as the new poor law in 1834 and municipal corporations in 1835, Peel either actively supported the government or did not interfere. During 1837 and 1838, he supported the Whig legislation on various contentious Irish issues, including tithe and poor law reform. The Whig party manager, Edward Ellice, noted in 1836 that Peel 'was as anxious as the most selfish adherent of the Treasury to keep the Gov't in office'.

At the general elections of 1835 and 1847, the Tories improved their position substantially. They won about a hundred seats more in 1835 than during the disastrous post-reform election of 1832 and, having added about forty more in the election necessitated by the death of William IV, were only about thirty short of the Whigs and their normal voting allies in the years 1837–41. Many Tories felt that Peel should seek to turn out the Whig government at the earliest possible opportunity, with the help of dissident Radical votes in the Commons if necessary. The Tories were increasingly confident of ultimate success and by-elections between 1837 and 1841 seemed to confirm that the tide was running in their favour. They were, however, by no means united either on principles or on tactics. It was widely felt that Peel should have taken the opportunity presented in 1839 when Melbourne resigned after his government's majority on the Jamaica bill fell to five. They were concerned that Peel had upset the new Queen during the Bedchamber Crisis which followed (see above). It was feared that the image of a young monarch browbeaten by an experienced and arrogant politician – however at variance with the truth – would alienate popular support and convince voters that Queen Victoria's preference for the Whigs, and her partiality for the avuncular Lord Melbourne, was well grounded.

Ireland was another bone of contention. Votes on Irish issues, especially in the Lords where the nominal Tory leader Baron Lyndhurst was no friend of Peel's, showed the extent of Tory divisions, but dissident Tory votes in the Commons were not uncommon. The myth that the Whigs were first humiliated and then destroyed in 1841 by a united Tory party needs to be dispelled.

By 1841, Peel had every reason to be grateful both for the inadequacies of Whig financial strategy and for the downswing in the economy which seemed to buttress his charges of financial mismanagement. Government deficits were reaching alarming proportions and Peel's financial expertise afforded him gratifying victories in debate over the Chancellor of the Exchequer, Sir Francis Baring. In 1841, fearful that if they did not make a move Peel might pre-empt them, the Whigs introduced a budget which promised general reductions in tariffs and less protection for farmers from a revised Corn Law. Their supporters in the towns, especially in the West Riding of Yorkshire, urged that these reforms would bring cheap bread and prosperity to the working classes.

With considerable effrontery, given the way his own mind was working and the course his government would shortly take (see Chapter 8), Peel savaged Baring's proposals: 'Can there be a more lamentable spectacle than that of a Chancellor of the Exchequer, seated on an empty chest, by the pool of bottomless deficiency, fishing for a budget?' The debate ended with a government defeat and, most gratifyingly in view of recent party indiscipline, only one Tory MP voted in support of the Whigs. A Tory motion of no confidence in the government followed almost immediately and on 5 June 1841 was won (like the next no-confidence defeat, that of James Callaghan's Labour government in 1979) by a single vote.

The Whigs, seeking to limit the damage, had already decided to risk their fortune at a general election, but being forced to hold it after the Commons had declared no confidence in their capacity to govern gave the Tories a great psychological boost. To the reasons for increasing Tory success between 1832 and 1841, and to the great electoral victory of that year, we must now turn.

6
Revival: Toryism into Conservatism, 1832–41

When Peel hurriedly returned from Italy at the end of 1834 to form his first government, a letter from his close friend and political colleague Henry Goulburn awaited him. Goulburn explained the political climate during Peel's absence: 'the property of the Country desires a conservative & not an *ultra Tory* government, meaning by that a Government deaf to all improvement which comprises change, however much on other grounds to be desired'.

It is unlikely that this report came as any surprise to Peel. His own perception, at least since 1832, had been that those with property to conserve, many of them very recently enfranchised, wanted stability and sound government above all but recognized that purblind resistance to justified change was the surest prescription for disorder. The riots and alarms of 1830–2, furthermore, had provided ample evidence that this disorder could be on a sufficient scale to threaten the political system and advance 'the democratical spirit'.

Peel had a clear strategy for the revival of Toryism, based on broadening its electoral appeal and making it, as observers in our own age might say, more 'relevant' to the needs of a society changing with unprecedented rapidity. Much has been made of this. Not so much has been made of Peel's parliamentary strategy. He did not envisage significantly broadening the parliamentary party. Revived Toryism in Parliament would depend on a rapprochment between the 'administrative' or 'Court' Tories – professional politicians committed to the service of the monarch in the interests of the nation – and 'landed Tories', who represented rural England and distrusted change in general and strong central executives in particular. These Tories were the inheritors of what was called in the eighteenth century the 'country party' tradition. Peel did not envisage the election of substantial numbers of industrialists from the urban areas.

Peel's grand political design was not conceived primarily in party terms. Party was a necessary, but only subordinate, element. His overriding objective, both in Ireland and in Britain, was to yoke propertied interests decisively to the security of the old constitution. For him, propertied interests included industry and commerce and it was crucial to his strategy to preserve the landowners from breaking themselves on the wheel of narrow reaction. He believed that he was saving the Ultras from the certain destruction to which their own narrow perceptions of the national interest would condemn them.

Though he was reluctant to admit it, however, he needed the Ultras. By no means all of the old landed Tory party was anti-reformist, but it was impossible to revive the party's fortunes without first obtaining at least the grudging support of those who accused him of desertion in 1829. The King's dismissal of the Whigs in November 1834 (Chapter 5) gave Peel an ideal opportunity to do this by offering the Tories office once again. He used it to request a dissolution of parliament and to make a direct appeal to the new electorate.

The Tamworth Manifesto of December 1834 was the form which appeal took. Although addressed only to his Staffordshire constituents, it was in reality intended for nationwide distribution and discussion. Published election addresses by candidates to their constituents were already common but the novelty of the Tamworth Manifesto lay with its national coverage. According to Norman Gash, the Manifesto represented 'an electioneering document on a grand and unprecedented scale'. What is generally remembered about the Manifesto is its commitment to moderate reform. Peel promised 'a careful review of institutions, civil and ecclesiastical, undertaken in a friendly temper, combining with the firm maintenance of established rights, the correction of proved abuses and the redress of real grievances'. In this spirit, Peel committed his party to accepting parliamentary reform, while rejecting democracy.

The Manifesto was addressed to those without firm party loyalties: 'that great and intelligent class of society . . . which is much less interested in contentions of party, than in the maintenance of order and the cause of good government'. This, rightly, has been interpreted as a bid for middle-class votes and for broadening Tory appeal. However, the Tamworth Manifesto also aimed to appeal to all but the most bigoted Ultras. Establishing a tradition for later election appeals, the Manifesto was much better on fine-sounding generalities than on commitment to specific policy but it did make concrete proposals for reviving the fortunes of the Church of England by reforming its most irritating and irrational abuses, such as the holding of more than one living by a single cleric and the grotesque disparity of income between richer and poorer clergy.

This section of the Manifesto was designed to convince Ultras, whose commitment to the Church of England was at the heart of their belief in the primacy of a Protestant constitution in Church and State, that Peel the emancipator of the Catholics was first and foremost a committed Church of England man. Peel's brief minority government of 1834–5 achieved nothing in legislative terms except the establishment of the Ecclesiastical Commission. From the Commission's recommendations, however, flowed the legislation passed by the Whigs between 1836 and 1840 which was responsible for buttressing the Church and fighting off radical demands for Disestablishment.

The Manifesto had the dual aim of widening Tory support in the country and convincing Peel's opponents within the party that he had their interests at heart. The substantially increased Tory vote in the 1835 election suggests that the former purpose was successful. Peel had some success in the latter also. Some Ultras branded the Manifesto dangerously 'liberal' but the majority were prepared to accept Peel's leadership, and with it his interpretation of Toryism, though guardedly. By 1835, as the more perceptive of them saw, they had little alternative to Peel. The Ultras and other landed Tories were leaderless and anyway in considerable need of political rehabilitation, so Peel's ecclesiastical olive branch could be seized gratefully enough. The landed Tories would neither love nor fully trust Peel. For the moment, however, they were happy to follow him.

The attempt to broaden the party base was accompanied by the gradual adoption of the term 'Conservative' in place of 'Tory'. The MP Sir John Welsh explained his understanding of the distinction in 1836: 'The Conservative party is not identical with the Tory party. It includes, indeed, the Tories, but it is a more comprehensive term and the basis is a wider one . . . the Conservative party may be said to consist of all that part of the community who are attached to the constitution in *Church* and *State* and who believe that it is threatened with subversion by the encroachments of democracy.' Despite this helpful distinction, however, the terms 'Conservatives' and 'Tories' continued to be used interchangeably in common parlance.

The Conservatives made substantial progress between the end of 1834 and the famous general election victory of 1841. Why did they recover so quickly? Various explanations have been offered but perhaps too much of this success has been attributed to Peel's leadership, both by contemporaries and by some later historians. The *Annual Register* of 1839 personalized the issue: 'No man, it is probable, ever deserved better of a party than Sir Robert Peel of his. . . . Unassisted by the faculties, the temperate wisdom and the parliamentary tactic and address of their leader in the House of Commons, they [the Tories] could scarcely . . . have recovered with such steady rapidity, and with so few reverses from the prostration in which the revolutionary struggle of 1831 and 1832 had left them.' Norman Gash considered that 'Peel's restraint and realism . . . enlarged and consolidated the forces of Conservatism'. Yet there is a sense in which Tory recovery after 1832 was almost inevitable. As Gash himself acknowledged: 'Many forces had been at work and most of them had little or nothing to do with Peel.' It is worth examining these in a little more detail.

First, the depth of the Tory trough after the 1832 election is easily overstated. That election was untypical in almost every respect, and not least because it became almost a retrospective plebiscite on the desirability of parliamentary reform. Many Tory candidates sacrificed themselves needlessly beyond this last ditch. What appeared to be an enormous Whig majority did not produce a massive, committed or united Whig party so much as a loose agglomeration of reform supporters. Once that dust settled, the fragility of the basis for common action on the Whig side became apparent. About forty MPs who had supported the Reform Act crossed over to the Conservative side between the elections of 1832 and 1837.

Second, the relationship between the core of the Whig party, led by grandees such as Grey, Melbourne, Russell and Lansdowne, and the exotic assortment of radical politicians was only a marriage of temporary convenience. Melbourne had absolutely nothing in common, either ideologically or socially, with nationalists like O'Connell or democratic currency reformers like the Birmingham banker Thomas Attwood. From the earliest years, the apparently secure Whig majority was in reality fragile. Once Peel had established his strategy of 'government in opposition', the Whigs often depended on Tory votes to sustain 'sensible' measures against radical pressure. The Whigs, therefore, were never as strong as their majorities implied and the core of their party had scarcely greater parliamentary support in the 1830s, than in the long years of parliamentary opposition to Lord Liverpool between 1812 and 1827.

The signs of marital strain between Whigs and Radicals soon appeared. O'Connell's supporters were anxious to press the Irish cause, and discontent flared once again in the early 1830s. The Whig response to this was a mixture of coercion and attempted reform. Since this reform involved using surplus Church of Ireland (Irish Anglican) revenues for a range of educational and social purposes, it stirred deep passions. Churchmen hated the idea of using Church money for any State purpose, and it was not only committed Tories who saw this apparently benign initiative as the thin end of a wedge which would end with Disestablishment and the destruction of Church supremacy. The 'Appropriation' issue, as it was called, considerably weakened the Whig government and precipitated the resignation of four Cabinet ministers in June 1834. Two of these, Edward Stanley (later Earl of Derby) and Sir James Graham, after a few years of ineffectual attempts to create a centre party, had become Conservative supporters by the late 1830s and would serve with distinction in Peel's famous government of 1841–6.

The Church question, therefore, provided a convenient rallying point for a reviving Tory party. Peel exploited his opportunity with skill, but the opportunity itself had been provided by the Whigs. From concern over the Church, it was only a short step to worries about the Whigs' ability to safeguard all property. The 1832 Reform Act had substantially widened the electoral base, but virtually all the new electors were small property owners. None are so tenacious in their defence of property as those who have relatively little of it and thus feel threatened by the ambitions of those just below them. As Michael Brock observed in his study of the Reform Act, modest property owners, having achieved the vote in 1832, did not greatly favour 'further adventures'. Yet such adventures seemed much more likely with the Whigs than with the Tories.

This was especially so after April 1835 when, after a general election in which they had lost support, the Whig leadership felt it necessary to make the so-called 'Lichfield House Compact' with assorted Radicals and O'Connellite Irishmen. The Compact's purpose was to secure a majority in the Commons to get rid of Peel's government. This was entirely successful in the short term. However, the longer-term implications for the Whigs were anything but happy. The Compact was the first formal agreement between the Whigs, Radicals and nationalists. In England, at least, the strong probability is that it alienated more voters than it attracted, precisely because it seemed to presage 'further adventures'. Whether these comprised more concessions to those who wanted to dismantle the Anglo-Irish Union, a weakening of the Church of England, a system of education controlled by State rather than Church, a secret ballot or votes for the working classes, the electorate as a whole was at least sceptical, if not downright fearful, rather than enthusiastic.

In the circumstances, Peel's pledge that the Reform Act should be seen as 'the final settlement of a great constitutional question' had a sympathetic resonance. Significantly, Tory propaganda in the later 1830s tended to stress the Whigs' inability to restrain wild figures to their left. Sir James Graham, in an effective speech at Merchant Taylor's Hall in 1838, for example, asserted that the Reform Act was as far as sensible men would want to go but that his old Whig allies could no longer be trusted to hold the line against damaging further changes in Church and State.

Peel's cause was further advanced by the frequency of general elections in the 1830s. These enabled propertied opinion to be both canvassed and heard. The election of 1832 was necessitated by the Reform Act. After it, the next would not normally have been held until 1839. However, Peel used William IV's invitation to ask the Tories to form a minority government at the end of 1834 to request a dissolution of parliament and allow the Tories a chance to regroup, which they took. The 1837 election, which saw further Tory gains, came about only because of the death of William IV and the then requirement that a new monarch must have a new parliament. These elections undoubtedly boosted Tory morale, but their circumstances were fortuitous.

The case for arguing that a Tory revival was almost bound to take place is a strong one but does it tell the whole story? Without strong and clear-headed leadership, it might be argued, these gains could as easily have evaporated as been consolidated. Peel's handling of a difficult parliamentary situation during the brief minority government of December 1834 to April 1835 won almost universal praise.

The Times, admittedly a newspaper highly sympathetic to the Tories, gushed about 'temper, capacity and powers . . . absolutely unapproached by any Minister but one [the younger Pitt] who has addressed Parliament since the beginning of the present century'. Greville, more sceptical but worldly-wise and shrewd, commented on his 'great capacity' and 'safe views and opinions'. Peel was also absolutely the right man to capitalize on Whig financial difficulties during the growing economic crisis and periods of unemployment of 1838–41. At a time when evident control of a brief, debating skill and command of the House of Commons counted for far more than they do nowadays, Peel's parliamentary performances there greatly contributed to the Tory revival.

He was also well aware of the need for party organization. The 1832 Reform Act required electors to register their entitlement to vote. This presented an excellent opportunity for local supporters to organize and maximize their party's voting strength. Many aspects of modern party organization date from the 1830s and there is little doubt that, despite several exceptions in the larger boroughs where Liberals were particularly effective, the Conservatives were much the better organized national party. Peel urged his supporters, in a famous speech in 1837, to 'Register, register, register' and told his Tamworth constituents in 1841 that 'the battle of the constitution must be fought in the registration courts'.

It may legitimately be doubted, however, how much Tory organization owed to Peel. He made exhortations which were widely publicized, but the spadework was done by others – the party agent F. R. Bonham, and myriad local representatives working for the cause. Other Tories, like Archibald Alison, had spelled out the value of 'a good registration' before Peel took it up. His relations with the many local Tory organizations which sprang up after the government of 1834–5 were not particularly close and his aversion to extra-parliamentary pressure as well as his own shyness both contributed to the awkwardness of the relationship with loyal 'Operative Conservative Associations' of working men established in northern industrial towns.

A party leader who set such store on broadening the party's appeal should perhaps have responded with greater cordiality to expressions of support in the constituencies. But such a reaction would have been uncharacteristic. Anyone less like a populist politician it would be difficult to imagine. Peel was happy to leave detailed organizational work to others, believing that a party with a clear sense of direction would earn more willing support and thus anyway be easier to organize. He would provide the leadership; it was the responsibility of others to ensure that there would be sufficient followers.

Peel's leadership effectively capitalized on trends in the 1830s which anyway favoured a revival of Toryism. But were the Conservatives a party fashioned in Peel's image and what was the basis of the party's strength at the time he became prime minister a second time? To answer these questions, it is necessary to analyse the general election of 1841, one of the most significant in the nineteenth century.

7

The general election of 1841

Both John Wilson Croker, a leading Tory writer of the 1830s and 1840s, and the historian Norman Gash believe that the credit for the Tory victory of 1841 lies with Robert Peel. Croker stated in *The Quarterly Review* that 'Every Conservative candidate professed himself in plain words to be Sir Robert Peel's man, and on that ground was elected'. Gash believes that the election, including 'success in the urban constituencies', was a tribute to Peel's ability to broaden the Conservative appeal and 'practical reward for all that he had worked for in the previous decade'.

The 1841 election was, of course, a famous triumph. It produced a victory for the Conservatives by more than seventy seats and was also the first time in British electoral history that a party with at least a theoretical parliamentary majority had been replaced in government by another with a majority. Moreover, Queen Victoria, no lover of the Tories after years of careful tutelage from the outgoing

Table 1 The general election of 1841

	England	Wales	Scotland	Ireland	Total
Conservatives	281	21	22	43	367
Whigs/Liberals	190	8	31	62	291
Total	471	29	53	105	658

Conservative majority: 76.

Table 2 Percentage of seats won by Conservatives in each country

	%	No.
England	59.7	471
Wales	72.4	29
Scotland	41.5	53
Ireland	41.0	105

premier Lord Melbourne and especially after her embarrassing brush with Peel over the Bedchamber issue in 1839 (Chapter 5), had no leeway in the choice of the next prime minister. She must have Peel or no one since Peel, as party leader, was the electorate's choice. The election was a landmark in the development of party government.

But what kind of Conservative party had the electorate chosen and what was the significance of the victory for the role of party? The answers to these questions are, perhaps, not the ones which most of the textbooks lead us to expect. They also provide important clues to explaining why Peel's government, though full of administrative and financial successes as we shall see, was ultimately to prove such a political disaster.

At first sight, Table 3 seems to support the conclusions that Peel had broadened the Tory base. Conservatives won almost as many seats as the Liberals in the English and Welsh boroughs. For a 'party of the land' this was a notable achievement. Yet a look at what kinds of boroughs these were is instructive. Only forty-four of the seats won in English and Welsh boroughs were in places with electorates of 1,000 or more. In the fifty-eight largest boroughs, where the Liberals won almost three times as many seats as the Conservatives, Peel's party suffered a net loss of two compared with its performance in the 1837 election. These large boroughs, of course, were concentrated in the industrial midlands and north – precisely where Peel was seeking to broaden the party's electoral base. Yet it was here that

Table 3 Analysis of the election according to type of seat

	English boroughs & universities	English counties	Welsh boroughs	Welsh counties	Scottish boroughs	Scottish counties
Conservatives	157	124	8	13	2	20
Whigs/Liberals	170	20	6	2	21	10

Table 4 Analysis of the election in English boroughs

	Large English boroughs (more than 2,000 electors)	Medium English boroughs (1,000– 2,000 electors)	Small English boroughs (fewer than 1,000 electors
Conservatives	15	29	109
Whigs/Liberals	43	34	93

the Conservatives did least well. Those larger towns in which they did have some success were older ports and commercial centres like the City of London, Bristol and Hull rather than industrial textile giants like Manchester or Leeds.

In general, the Conservatives did best in those boroughs which had been least changed by the 1832 Reform Act. Several of these were still old-style 'rotten boroughs' where the patronage of a substantial landowner, rather than electoral popularity, was the decisive factor. Here elections still followed a recognizably eighteenth-century pattern; actual contests were a rarity and members frequently returned unopposed. Many had little or nothing to do with industry, being market towns whose economy depended on agriculture. It is not often remarked that the 1841 general election, apparently the triumphant vindication of Peel's 'broadening' strategy, saw actual contests in only 47 per cent of the country's constituencies, considerably less than in the elections of 1832, 1835 and 1837, which the Whigs/Liberals won, albeit with dwindling majorities.

The Conservative majority of 1841, therefore, was based in the smaller boroughs and, especially, in the counties of England. Indeed, the Liberals were all but wiped out in the English counties, winning only twenty (14 per cent) of the 144 available seats. By contrast, Scotland and Ireland both returned Whig or Whig-allied majorities of roughly three to two. The Conservatives hardly made any kind of showing in the Scottish boroughs.

The Conservatives won in 1841 because they had majority support where the seats were thickest on the ground (southern England), not where the electorates were most numerous or most changed by recent industrial and commercial developments. The Conservatives were the party of rural England and its small market towns: squirearchical, deferential, Church-loving, intolerant of any diversity of religious view, and much keener to preserve the past than look to the future. They were not strong in the United Kingdom as a whole. Despite Peel's best endeavours, his Conservative party remained dominated by old-style Tory opinion.

An analysis of candidates' statements and speeches and of the newspaper reports relating to the election confirms this assessment. In many constituencies, as was the case at least until 1867, the election turned mainly on local issues, personalities or loyalties. When national policy predominated, the issues which brought out the Tory vote were economic protection for the landed interest and defence of the Church. There was widespread fear in the shires of the Whigs' intention to modify the Corn Laws and thus to jeopardize agricultural protection. The effect of Francis Baring's recent budget, warned the Tory *Kentish Gazette* in May 1841, would be to 'overthrow the existing order of society, to trample down the agriculturalist and the farm labourer'. The same calculations almost certainly enabled the Whig–Liberals to hold on to many of their prized northern industrial seats. It was also widely suggested that removing protection would also harm commercial interests, increase unemployment and reduce wages. Ironically, in view of what was to happen during Peel's government, Tory votes appear to have been cast overwhelmingly for the party most likely to protect landowners and defend the Protestant established Church.

Significantly, Peel did little to advertise either to voters or to his supporters his own unease about Protection. He relied on his growing reputation as an expert on financial and commercial affairs to give him votes in the towns, while encouraging rural Tories to let rip in defence of the Corn Laws and 'old England' more generally. Melbourne's Whigs undoubtedly looked the more vulnerable because of the sharpness of Peel's attacks on the mounting government deficit but the wider economic problems, which were at their peak in 1841, contributed to the Whig defeat.

Not surprisingly, a large number of the Conservative MPs elected in 1841 were fervent Protectionists. Peel certainly had a broader vision, but his party's creed was much narrower than his own. The new prime minister had no right to expect either that his followers were converts to economic liberalism or, on the evidence of their speeches, that they could be converted to free trade. The reformist elements so prominent in the Tamworth Manifesto of 1834 hardly featured in the literature of 1841. Protectionist arguments were very prominent and carried the day where they were most likely to – in rural England. It has to be said, also, that Peel – by now going all out for electoral victory and a return to office – did little or nothing to inform potential Tory voters of his real intentions in economic policy. Accordingly, the 1841 general election was properly a victory for Protectionist Toryism, not Peelite Conservatism. Yet much of Peel's policy as prime minister between 1841 and 1846 ignored this crucial distinction. The line of causation from the 'triumph' of 1841 to the 'disaster' of 1846 is clearly traceable.

8

Executive government under Peel, 1841–6

'I am told that in the exercise of power . . . I must be the instrument of maintaining the opinions and feelings which I myself am disposed to repudiate. With my views of Government . . . the obligations which it imposes, the duties which it entails, the sacrifices it involves – I am not disposed to add to these sacrifices, by accepting it with a degrading and dishonourable condition. . . . If I exercise power, it shall be upon my conception – perhaps imperfect, perhaps mistaken – but my sincere conception of public duty.'

The words of Sir Robert Peel in the Commons immediately after the 1841 election which would shortly bring him to power. It was the clearest possible declaration on his view of the relationship between political parties and the exercise of power. For Peel, in 1841 as it was to be in 1846, party had an entirely subordinate function. His conception was that the prime minister should do his public duty on behalf of the sovereign and in the interests of the nation. It was the duty of the party to submit to these higher imperatives. Peel, therefore, felt entirely justified in his lofty pronouncement that, if agricultural protection were proved to be at the root of the country's current financial troubles, he would ask the landowners to make a 'sacrifice' by earnestly advising 'a relaxation, an alteration, nay, if necessary a repeal, of the corn laws'.

His Tory backbenchers would have been entitled to ask why, if his mind was really open on the Corn Laws, he had allowed them to pile up votes in the shires on support for agricultural protection which Whig–Liberal proposals threatened (see Chapter 10). They would have been entitled to ask whether Peel would have won power had it not been for the result of an election fought substantially on the Protection question. Anxious to see the back of the Whigs and to re-establish a majority Tory government for the first time in more than a decade, they did neither of these things. Peel, for the moment, got away with his claim to unfettered freedom of political action while the long fuse of party frustration, which would lead to the explosion of 1846, remained to be lit. His position was, to put it at its kindest, paradoxical. He had used a revived Conservative party as the vehicle to gain power. He now sought to rule as an expert above the fray of party battle. As Dr Hawkins has neatly described it, the Tory victory of 1841 was 'a great party triumph for an anti-party view of executive authority'. Peel from 1841 was an executive prime minister, not a party leader.

His choice of Cabinet reflected his priorities. He kept faith with most of those who had served in his brief minority government of 1834–5 but he was careful to find important positions for Sir James Graham (Home Secretary) and Viscount Stanley (War and the Colonies). They were the two leading defectors from the Whigs in 1834 and men already of proven ability. The Presidency of the Board of Trade, a vital commercial post, went to the Earl of Ripon, a close colleague (as F. J. Robinson) from the 1820s and now, despite his fatuous interlude as prime minister in 1827–8, one of the great survivors of Tory politics.

Wellington survived from the 1820s too, but with his faculties somewhat impaired by age (in 1841 he was 72). A combination of increasing deafness and permanent lack of tact would have made him an unwise choice as Foreign Secretary, the post he had briefly held in 1834–5. Peel was happy to see him in Cabinet with the largely honorific title of Minister without Portfolio. This enabled him to return the Earl of Aberdeen to the Foreign Secretaryship, a post he had held between 1828 and 1830 in Wellington's government. A cautious, conscientious and fastidious man, Aberdeen had been schooled in diplomacy by the Younger Pitt; Peel, whose own interest in foreign affairs was not pronounced, was happier to delegate responsibility here than in any other aspect of government work.

To the Chancellorship of the Exchequer, where precisely the opposite situation obtained, Peel appointed his old friend and close confidant Henry Goulburn, knowing that he could rely on conscientious and effective discharge of his own policies from that quarter. Outside the Cabinet, Peel gave his first taste of government office to William Gladstone, later the nineteenth century's pre-eminent Liberal prime minister but in 1841 still, as the Whig historian T. B. Macaulay termed him, 'the rising hope of the stern, unbending Tories'. Gladstone, whose abilities were already recognized as being rivalled only by his conscience, became Ripon's deputy and took over from him, with his first Cabinet post, when the latter moved to the Board of Control in 1843.

Peel's was an administration fashioned for executive efficiency. Virtually the only concession made to party sentiment was the appointment of the Duke of Buckingham, self-appointed leader of the agricultural interest, to the anyway largely titular post of Lord Privy Seal. Buckingham, who had a large ego but was not cut out for detailed administrative work, was, as Gash put it, 'the darling of the Buckinghamshire farmers' and Peel's hope was that this solitary Protectionist flag would deflect the backbench breezes of criticism away from an administration dedicated to doing the nation good.

No doubt existed in Peel's mind as to the best way of doing the nation good. His administration before the Corn Law crisis of 1845–6 is mostly remembered for its economic and fiscal reforms. 'The Condition of England question', as it was called, public order, and Irish affairs were not unimportant but always yielded in priority to the need to make the country solvent and prosperous. No one with a knowledge of Peel would find this priority in the least strange. He believed that the only route to social harmony was via economic progress, and he believed that the only route to economic progress was by treading the path of financial probity and rectitude. This involved keeping government cheap and wealth-generators happy and productive. He justified scepticism about any wider political philosophy by reference to its cost. 'Philosophers are very regardless of expense when the public has to bear it', he tartly informed his First Lord of the Admiralty, the Earl of Haddington, in 1844. He had earlier declared to the House of Commons that 'Of all the vulgar arts of government that of solving every difficulty which might arise by thrusting the hand into the public purse is the most delusory and contemptible'.

Priority, accordingly, had to be given to finance. According to Gash, 'at the heart of Peel's policy was the conviction that the only way to overcome both the human misery and the social threat was to increase the purchasing power of the masses'. If the country were prosperous, in other words, social tension would be reduced. The equation was too simple, but the experience of mid-Victorian Britain, when the so-called 'Hungry Forties' were past, suggests that it contained an essential truth.

Peel's first concern was to eliminate the government deficit run up by the Whigs during the economic depressions at the end of their period in office. The budget of 1842, which he introduced in a speech lasting almost four hours, was the chosen instrument. Income tax was reintroduced at 7d (3p) in the pound on incomes of more than £150. This threshold was carefully chosen to ensure that virtually none of the working classes had to pay it. The tax was designed to last for three years and to contribute £3.7 million towards new revenue of £4 million raised to eliminate the deficit. By contrast, customs duties were reduced on about 750 of 1,200 items. The maximum import duty on raw materials was set at 5 per cent and on manufactured items 20 per cent. A new, and reduced, scale of duties was introduced for corn.

The budget was controversial but politically well judged. Peel asked the wealthier classes to make an additional contribution, in the form of income tax, during an economic crisis so that the 'labouring classes of society' might not be further burdened. As this appeal was made near the time of substantial disturbances by Chartists who were agitating to have the vote given to all men, it is not surprising that the middle and upper classes might consider their self-interest better served by a small additional temporary tax burden than by resisting the income tax and risking popular disturbances. Approval for what the diarist Greville grandly called 'this just measure, so lofty in conception, right in direction and able in execution' greatly outran disapproval and criticism on the Conservative benches was strangely muted, even over the reduction in corn duties. Buckingham, however, could not stomach this and resigned from the Cabinet.

The Budget as a whole is best seen as a continuation of the trade liberalization initiatives developed by Robinson and Huskisson in the 1820s. Except for the income tax and the decisiveness and *élan* with which it was introduced, its broad direction was remarkably similar to the Baring budget of 1841 which Peel had taken such delight in savaging (see Chapter 5). As in the days of Pitt, the income tax proved relatively easy to collect and also lucrative. Trade revived from 1843 onwards and the stimulus to consumption provided by reduced duties soon outran the lower tariff return on each item. Government finances moved into surplus in 1844.

The overall philosophy apparently vindicated, Peel proceeded in 1845 to introduce even more sweeping measures of trade liberalization. Income tax, a temporary measure to ease the country through economic crisis in 1842, had miraculously become for Peel 'the foundation of the commercial policy of the country' by 1845 and was renewed for a further three years. By 1845, it was not only inveterate cynics who assumed that the tax would become permanent, as, despite Gladstone's best efforts in the 1870s, it did. Raising about £5.5 million in the later 1840s, it was soon providing about 10 per cent of government income. The 1845 budget was even more swingeing in its reduction of duties. Those on raw cotton went entirely, as did duties on most raw materials. Controversially, given the number of Conservative supporters in the large ports, duties on colonial sugar from the West Indies and on foreign sugar were both reduced. Further reductions followed and by the time of the government's fall in 1846, Britain had become an almost completely free-trading nation.

The other central pillar of Peel's fiscal reforms was the Bank Charter Act of 1844. Peel considered this one of his most important legislative achievements, ensuring that the issuing of notes remained related to reserves of gold. The Act, which has been criticized by economic historians as resting on both a naïve and an outmoded defence of the principles of 'bullionism' (see Chapter 3), defined the role of the Bank of England in the British economy carefully. Its ability to issue promissary notes in place of cash was confirmed but issues in excess of £14 million had to be backed by bullion reserves. The rights of other English banks to issue their own notes were restricted and, as the century progressed, the Bank of England came to have virtually a monopoly of English note issues.

The Act confirmed the triumph of 'bullionists', of whom none was more rigidly orthodox than Peel, over 'paper currency' theorists like Thomas Attwood and Thomas Tooke who were groping towards a mechanism to ensure stability of prices in a rapidly expanding but volatile economy. Peel never had any time for such, as he saw it, dangerous tinkering with the currency. His speech to the Commons made it clear that the Act's main purpose was 'to inspire just confidence in the medium of exchange'. It remained the basis of British currency control until the First World War.

Peel's unequivocal belief was that the government's main concern with the 'social question' should be in helping to provide the economic conditions which would stimulate economic growth, create new jobs and enable ordinary folk to consume more. Direct government intervention to 'solve' social problems was likely to be counterproductive and was anyway far less efficient than free-market solutions. Government action, therefore, should be slender, subordinate and supportive of other initiatives. In 1842, for example, his government extended the Whig 1834 Poor Law Amendment Act and upheld its controversial basic strategy of making poor relief demeaning to seek and thus 'less eligible' than independent wage labour. The Act also enabled a check to be made on 'wasteful' expenditure by ratepayers and offered an incentive for paupers to help themselves out of their plight.

For Peel, 'government social policy' was a contradiction in terms. He was neither heartless nor mean, although in the normal currency of political debate, his opponents accused him of being both. He was a wealthy Christian gentleman who believed in charity as the proper way of alleviating short-term distress. In the longer term, charity should be supplemented by education and other constructive means towards making people self-sufficient. He made numerous charitable donations, many of them anonymous, during the long period of high unemployment and rising prices between 1837 and 1842.

Government support for social measures was, therefore, unlikely to be fervent. Nevertheless, a fine head of steam about 'the social question' was building up outside parliament in response both to parliamentary reports originally commissioned by the Whigs in the late 1830s and to extra-parliamentary agitation for a range of humanitarian causes espoused both by radical politicians and by Tory paternalists unpersuaded of the benefits of industrial capitalism. The Mines Act of 1842, which forbade the employment of women and children in mining activities beneath ground, was not government legislation. It reached the statute book thanks to the lobbying of Viscount Ashley (later Seventh Earl of Shaftesbury) and the heightening of public consciousness following revelations about the conditions under which children had to work. The government provided assistance in drafting the legislation but did not take the initiative.

Factory proposals introduced by the government proved controversial. Graham's attempt to reduce the hours worked by women and children in 1843 was linked to proposals for compulsory schooling provided, in most instances, by the Church of England. In the face of unremitting hostility from nonconformists and the feeling that a measure which should have wide public support was becoming unacceptably partisan, the bill was withdrawn. In the following year, shorn of its education clauses, Graham's Factory Bill proposed to reduce the maximum working day for children to six hours, only to be confronted by a well-orchestrated campaign, with both Whig and Tory paternalist support in Parliament and effective press lobbying outside, to restrict the maximum working day for all to ten hours. The 'Ten Hours Campaign' had been active since the early 1830s and by 1844 it had mobilized substantial support both in parliament and outside on both humanitarian and practical grounds. How could efficiency and safety be preserved among workers forced to work for longer?

Peel dissented. The measure was, of course, contrary to his political philosophy, dependent as it was upon the free play of market forces. Women and children were not, in the eyes either of the law or practical family arrangements, free to choose their jobs. Government might thus properly acknowledge a responsibility to protect them from exploitation. Adult males, however, were free agents and legislation must not presume to alter what market forces dictated. If an employer, required by law to reduce working hours, became uncompetitive and had to lay off workers, where was the advantage for the employee? Sensitive though he was to humanitarian arguments, he nevertheless told the Commons that the proposed Ten Hours maximum would deprive textile owners of the equivalent of seven weeks' work during the year. Since textiles accounted for approximately 80 per cent of all British exports in the 1840s, the effect on Britain's trade recovery was bound to be severe. 'I admit', said Peel, 'that I am afraid of foreign competition.'

Peel's fears were insufficient to persuade the Commons, which voted to accept Ashley's Ten Hours' Amendment. Reluctant Tories were only persuaded to change their minds by Peel's crude threat to resign. Graham's 1844 Factory Act effectively set a maximum working day at twelve hours. Ten Hours Legislation had to await the return of a Liberal government and was enacted in 1847.

By 1844, Peel's disagreements with his backbenchers were becoming both frequent and acrimonious. On the social question, on religion, on trade, on education and on Ireland, Peel seemed to landed Tories to be going his own way, certain of his own policies, buttressed by a coterie of like-minded ministers and apparently impervious to criticism. The decisive conflict between an 'executive' minister and a frustrated party was beginning to take shape.

9

Peel and backbench Toryism, 1841–5

As an examination of the 1841 election suggests (Chapter 7), Peel's victorious Conservative party was not naturally sympathetic to free trade ideas. Peel's difficulties with his backbenchers stemmed not just from ideological differences but also from different conceptions both of party and the nature of political loyalty. Peel in office saw himself as the Queen's minister discharging his responsibilities according to the national interest. It was part of his responsibility to interpret what the national interest was. Backbench Tories largely interpreted the national interest as the landed interest writ large and buttressed by the Church of England.

Peel in office took the view that this was too narrow a basis not only for legislative action but also for a national party. Yet, as recently as 1838, in a speech at Merchant Taylors' Hall he had said that Conservatism should defend establishment institutions: 'By conservative principles I mean a determination to resist every encroachment that can curtail the just rights and settled privileges of one or other of those three branches of the state [King, Lords and Commons]. . . . there shall be an established religion and an imperishable faith, and that established religion shall maintain the doctrines of the Protestant Church. By conservative principles I mean, a steady resistance to every project which would divert church property from strictly spiritual uses, a determination to meet every threatened danger to the Protestant establishment.'

Perhaps this was a plea for support from Tories who had not

trusted Peel since 1829 rather than a statement of faith. However, he did little between 1838 and the election of 1841 to dissuade Tories from believing that his Conservatism matched theirs. He allowed supporters to exploit the Whigs' desire to reform the Corn Laws (Chapter 10) which were such an article of faith for country gentlemen, and informed his Tamworth electors that the country's distresses were not attributable to the operation of agricultural protection. Conservative supporters went to the polls in 1841 believing that their leader was an anti-reformer in all essentials. If the theme of the Tamworth Manifesto had been the need to reform in order to conserve, that of the Merchant Taylors' speech was that the necessary reforms had been completed or were in train.

Peel's speech immediately after the election, which effectively discharged him from any prior obligations (see Chapter 8), represented, at the very least, an important shift of emphasis. Tory backbenchers, still euphoric after their election victory, would have done well to heed its implications. In office, Peel rarely considered their wishes; he either assumed the unswerving loyalty of Conservatives in Parliament or evinced indignant irritation when it was not forthcoming.

Strains between Peel and his backbenchers were apparent from the outset. The 1842 budget produced pointed criticisms from the shires. George Palmer, the MP for South Essex, for example, was concerned that the movement towards free trade would not stop until it swept the Corn Laws clean away. Conservative whips warned Peel that his policy was not welcomed, and in one budget division no fewer than eighty-five Conservatives failed to support him.

The poor law and factory reform were also issues which detached a substantial minority of Tory MPs from the leadership. It has been estimated that fifty-three Conservatives, mostly representing northern constituencies, saw it as their duty to oppose the continuation of the hated poor law of 1834 and to support a compulsory maximum ten-hour day for factory workers. They could not threaten Peel's position but they acted both as a permanent irritant in the early years of the ministry and as an embarrassing reminder in 1841–3 that cracks in Conservative unity were only being papered over. As *Fraser's Magazine* noted in September 1843: 'whether it be from pride, or shyness, or an excess of caution, the minister takes no pains whatever to win the personal love and affection of his supporters. As a party they are never admitted to his confidences.'

Party cracks widened damagingly in 1844, just as the long-standing government economic deficit was being turned around. Ninety-five Tories voted for Ashley's amendment to write a maximum ten-hour day into Graham's Factory Bill in March. This was substantially more than the complement of 'Tory Radicals' and paternalists and it precipitated a government defeat. In June, as part of its now well-advanced trade liberalization policy, the government proposed to reduce the duty on foreign sugar by almost one half while leaving slave-grown sugar from the West Indies at the same level. Philip Miles, the Conservative MP for Bristol, a port whose prosperity was closely linked to the West Indies trade, organized resistance and received support from sixty-one Tories. His amendment, like Ashley's, also passed.

Peel had no difficulty in reversing both decisions, but the manner of his doing so caused considerable offence. He refused to negotiate or compromise with his backbenchers, offering them the alternative of withdrawing their amendments or forcing him to resign. He told Lady de Grey in June that government defeats weakened his authority. They also threatened to transfer the initiative from the government to parliament and, thus, to 'parties wholly irresponsible and much less informed than Ministers are or ought to be'. Criticism about Peel's aloofness, overbearing manner and personal coldness had also begun to swell. The MP for Pontefract, Richard Milnes, considered Peel's style of leadership 'absolutely indefensible. . . . He is asking from his party all the blind confidence the country gentlemen placed in Mr Pitt . . . without himself fulfilling any of the engagements on his side'. The Whig opposition, lacking cohesion and direction since the 1841 election defeat, might have recalled the prescient observation which had appeared in its political journal *Edinburgh Review* in 1840 that Peel's 'ostracism [from his party] may be distant, but to us it appears certain'.

The Conservatives thus entered 1845 with morale low and unity in jeopardy. In a rare moment of levity, Peel joked about his wish that someone would introduce a compulsory ten-hour day for ministers. The quip had a serious side. It was clear that the prime minister was over-working; it was not only critics and opponents who detected a new testiness modifying the traditional reserve. The lack of rapport between prime minister and backbenchers left the Conservatives poorly equipped to meet the specially divisive challenges which Ireland still offered.

Peel had dealt adequately enough in 1843 with the renewed discontent which had surfaced around Daniel O'Connell's campaign to have the Act of Union repealed. Violence, or the threat of violence, was a constant accompaniment to this campaign and the government, treading the thinnest of lines between necessary firmness and the need not to alienate potential Catholic support, had passed the Irish Arms Act, requiring all firearms to be registered with the authorities. O'Connell's proposed anti-Union mass meeting at Clontarf was interpreted by the government as an incitement to illegality and banned. O'Connell himself, despite assertions that he only sought separation by peaceful means, was arrested on a charge of conspiracy a little later and convicted by a Protestant jury of incitement to treason before being released on appeal in 1844.

As Peel knew, however, support for Irish nationalism could not be neutralized merely by decisive action against O'Connell, an ageing and increasingly disspirited nationalist leader. In any case, Peel's broader strategy rested more upon accommodation with Catholic property owners than upon coercion. Both the logic of the situation and Peel's own experience as Chief Secretary convinced him that a population more than 80 per cent Catholic could not be coerced or discriminated against indefinitely. Peel submitted a lengthy memorandum to his Cabinet early in 1844 in which he asserted that, while the maintenance of the Union was the overriding objective, equality of treatment for Protestant and Catholic citizens was necessary in order to persuade the Irish majority of the value of the Union. Though, as most historians now agree, the basic Irish problem was an economic one – inadequate growth in an overwhelmingly agricultural economy for sustaining a massively increased population – Peel's solution was religious. He wanted to make public declaration from Britain of the government's commitment to proper education for Irish Catholic citizens.

The key to the problem, in Peel's view, lay with the Catholic priests whose influence over the peasantry was very substantial. Most priests were educated in a seminary at Maynooth (Co. Kildare) which was underfunded and inadequately administered. Peel considered that 'the wit of man could not devise a more effectual method for converting them into sour, malignant demogogues, hostile to the law, from all the sympathies of low birth and kindred, living by agitation, inclined to it and fitted for it by our . . . penurious system of education'. His solution was virtually to treble the annual grant to the college, make that grant permanent and provide £30,000 for new buildings. This became the kernel of Peel's Maynooth Bill, presented to the Commons early in 1845.

Peel had anticipated trouble with his party over Maynooth, but not the ferocity of the opposition it engendered. For loyal Anglicans, bent on defence of the Protestant Constitution in Church and State, it was yet another Peelite betrayal. To the original perfidy of emancipation was now to be added a policy of Catholic appeasement, which included reducing the extent of patronage available to Protestants in Ireland, the Charitable Bequests Act of 1844, which made it easier for gifts to be made to the Catholic Church, and finally, with the Maynooth Bill, positive discrimination in favour of representatives of the Church of Rome. It had not gone unnoticed, either, that Peel and Graham had preferred to withdraw a Factory Bill in 1843 in the face of dissenter and Catholic opposition rather than fight for the supremacy of the Church of England by defending that Bill's pro-Anglican education clauses (see Chapter 8).

Over Maynooth, of course, Anglican Tories and Dissenters were united. Dissenters organized a campaign against the Bill which gathered a million and a quarter signatures on more than ten thousand petitions. As usual, Peel convinced the Cabinet of its appropriateness and long-term necessity, if not its short-term political value. Gladstone, however, ever the most upright, assertive and sanctimonious defender of Anglican supremacy in the Cabinet, resigned over Maynooth in January 1845. He was persuaded back to fight the Corn Law crisis in December, thus providing one of the few instances in politics of a rat returning to a sinking ship.

On the second reading of the Maynooth Bill, Peel managed to secure a small majority among Conservatives (159 votes to 147), but on the crucial third reading, after more acrimony, Conservative opponents outnumbered supporters by 149 votes to 148. For the first time, Peel had a majority in his own party against him. The Maynooth Bill was carried only because the Whigs, preferring to let their historic commitment to religious toleration outweigh the opposition of their Dissenting supporters, mostly voted for it.

By the middle of 1845, Peel was becoming fatalistic about the future of his administration. In an unavailing attempt to keep Gladstone in the government, he had privately conceded that the Maynooth proposals would 'very probably be fatal to the Government' but argued that they were right. He thus had a duty as the Queen's minister to put them before the nation. The same point was made, in suitably orotund language, to the Commons in May 1845. A government must retain 'the absolute right, without reference to the past and without too much regard for what party considerations must claim from them, to risk even the loss of confidence of their friends, rather than abstain from doing that which conviction tells them the present circumstances require'.

Peel, therefore, would not compromise with the 'Protestants' in his party and, assured of sufficient Whig support, he had no need to in order to get the Bill passed. Characteristically, however, he had discounted the possibility that his opponents might have equally strong arguments in support of their own 'conviction' – of the supremacy of the Church of England and its importance in preserving the old Constitution in Church and State. The Home Secretary Sir James Graham knew that over Maynooth the government had finally 'lost the slight hold which we ever possessed over the hearts and kind feelings of our followers'.

Perhaps more significantly, Peel's Tory opponents found over the Maynooth question a parliamentary spokesman of verve, subtlety and ruthless opportunism. Whereas their parliamentary performances before 1845 had been characterized by a combination of choleric outrage and inarticulate passion in defence of the Constitution, their protests were now given a new, and more dangerous, dimension. Anyone less representative of the beating heart of rural England than Benjamin Disraeli it would be difficult to imagine. Disraeli was the son of a Jewish intellectual and was determined to make himself famous. He had written tolerably popular, and tolerably good, novels and had espoused romantic Tory causes loosely arranged around the conceit that the industrial revolution had not happened. He was extremely clever and utterly unscrupulous. The Liberal Quaker John Bright sardonically remarked that Disraeli was 'a self-made man and worships his creator'. Disraeli perceived in the disarray of the Conservative party in the mid-1840s his best chance to advance his political career. He seems to have had a personal grudge against Peel for refusing him office in 1841 when younger and better connected men, like Gladstone, had been preferred.

To champion the cause of the Tory opposition over Maynooth, therefore, seemed a natural career move for Disraeli. For the first time, Peel found a Tory opponent able and willing to make capital out of the broader issues thrown up by his proposals. In Disraeli's view, Peel was abusing his position as the head of a great party by going against the clear wishes of a majority of his supporters. Since the Commons was sustained by a government and an opposition which offered policies for the electorate to adjudicate upon, it was unacceptable for the leader of one party to shake off party obligations and arrogate to himself the right of speaking for the nation. Peel was lambasted as 'a great Parliamentary middleman . . . who bamboozles one party, and plunders the other'. Disraeli called for an end to 'this dynasty of deception' which had placed 'the intolerable yoke of official despotism' around the neck of parliament.

Disraeli and Peel had diametrically different views of the role of party in the parliamentary system. These arguments would be rehearsed yet more damagingly over the question of Corn Law repeal during the next two years. All of the ingredients for the collapse of the Conservative party were assembled by the time of the Maynooth vote. Peel was now to mix them to his own recipe.

10
The repeal of the Corn Laws and the fall of Peel

Many students find it strange that in 1846 a great political party should have broken up over a trading regulation. Considered in purely economic terms, of course, the Corn Laws amounted to precisely this. A simple explanation of their purpose, however, will quickly suggest that they had a far more important political resonance. The famous Corn Law of 1815 had been passed to ensure that, with food prices across Europe dropping sharply at the end of the Napoleonic Wars, British producers would have some protection against the dumping of large quantities of grain at rock-bottom prices.

From the beginning, this new law attracted criticism. Liverpool had tried to defend it as a measure which provided sufficient incentive for British farmers to continue production. It thus guarded against famine. Opponents characterized it in class terms. It was legislation designed to protect the landed interest. The cost of this inappropriate support was higher bread prices for ordinary working folk. Opposition to the Corn Laws became an important rallying cry for parliamentary reformers between 1815 and 1832.

For Peel, and what became known as 'liberal Tories' generally, the Corn Laws presented an acute dilemma. They were the evident obstacles to that freeing of trade restrictions on which, so the new political economy of Adam Smith and his followers held, economic growth and increased prosperity depended. On the other hand, they were embraced by the landed interest – which constituted the great bulk of Tory support – as the essential props of their survival. Protectionist Tories (as those who opposed the repeal of the Corn Laws were called) criticised Huskisson's and Peel's reductions of duty in their separate Corn Law amendments of 1828 and 1842 as detrimental to their interests. Abolition of the Corn Laws would be considered by many of Peel's supporters as the ultimate betrayal.

On the other side, failure to remove agricultural protection was increasingly regarded as a crime against the productive classes of the country. As Britain industrialized, so its population increased. Between 1801 and 1851 the population virtually doubled; these extra mouths had to be fed. Demographic pressures alone required that corn supplies be maximized, since bread was the staple diet. It became increasingly difficult to contest the argument that the Corn Laws protected a sector of the economy whose contribution to gross national product was lessening by the year while imposing heavy burdens on those who were contributing more and more. Employers complained that agriculture was receiving unfair, and unnecessary, protection to preserve the high levels of rent on which landowners lived. Rent, furthermore, was unearned income. Manufacturers on the other hand worked hard and took risks both to make their own profits and to provide work for their employees. Those employees had to pay more for bread than they would under free trade. In times of hardship especially, this was intolerable.

There is little doubt, as Boyd Hilton has argued, that Peel had become an intellectual convert to free trade as early as the 1820s. He had almost certainly made up his own mind before taking office in 1841 that, ultimately, the Corn Laws had to go. The question of repeal, therefore, was one of tactics and timing rather than overall strategy. The repeal of the Corn Laws was a natural extension of the policy of trade liberalization begun by William Pitt in the 1780s, continued by Robinson and Huskisson in the 1820s and accelerated by Peel's own budgets of 1842 and 1845. The new political economy, with its emphasis on trade liberalization and cheap government, was intellectually dominant by the 1840s. Every move towards complete free trade made the Corn Laws the more anomalous. Why, then, did Peel delay announcing his conversion to repeal until the end of 1845?

Several explanations can be offered but it is almost certain that the official reason given by the government – that repeal was necessary to cope with the consequences of the Irish potato famine – was not the real one. It is true that the failure of the Irish potato crop in 1845 and the imminent prospect of widespread famine presented Peel with a human crisis on a massive scale. With poor harvests throughout Europe and the certainty of higher food prices generally, it was unlikely that Englishmen would be able to afford the massive expenditure needed to stave off total catastrophe in Ireland. But immediate repeal would not enable sufficient supplies of food to be transferred to Ireland, and, even if changing the laws would help, Peel could have suspended their operation for the duration of the food crisis. Instead he moved immediately to total repeal. Suspension for the duration was urged on Peel by many of his opponents, and decisively rejected.

We should conclude that the Irish potato famine was the occasion, rather than the cause, of Corn Law repeal. Perhaps Peel would have preferred to 'sell' repeal to the public at the next election, due in 1847, but the famine of 1845 only accelerated his move by a year or so.

Three reasons probably explain why Peel did not move earlier. The first was party political. Like it or not, Peel stood at the head of a Protectionist party. He had given certain assurances to his supporters in the late 1830s and early 1840s which could not lightly be set aside. He had even encouraged Protectionists to attack the Whigs in 1841 on their unsoundness over agricultural protection. Besides, he wanted to remain prime minister and knew well that on Corn Law repeal a minister who had grievously disappointed his supporters before was especially vulnerable. His supporters would need to be persuaded gently and over a long period of time, if they were persuadable at all.

Second, the repeal of the Corn Laws was the primary objective of the Anti-Corn Law League, an overwhelmingly middle-class pressure group founded in Manchester in 1838 whose power base remained in the industrial north. It was well organized, extremely well funded and initiated a new development in British politics – a predominantly peaceful single-issue organization whose purpose was to coerce government into adopting its objective as policy. Peel regarded the Anti-Corn Law League with extreme distaste. He disliked 'single-issue' politics anyway but he particularly objected to the League's tactics. In 1841–2, though the League advocated peaceful protest, it was widely believed, not least by Graham who enquired into the question as Home Secretary, that its agitation had inflamed passions and contributed to the widespread industrial unrest with which he had to deal. League tactics were also considered by Peel to put members of parliament under inappropriate pressure.

64

It was the duty of government to settle matters as it saw best in the national interest. It should not be deflected from this course by the power of a sectional interest group. Peel believed that the League was attempting to usurp some of the functions of government in setting a highly specific political agenda.

The Anti-Corn Law League was at its height between 1838 and 1843 and it is likely that its very success dissuaded Peel from moving more quickly on repeal. He did not wish to risk being accused of acting under duress and thus sacrificing that integrity and independence of action which belonged uniquely to government. Peel's attitude may seem precious but it needs to be remembered that he was prime minister during a time of delicate transition from a predominantly agricultural to a predominantly commercial and industrial economy. He believed that the government should preserve traditional procedures during this transition, or risk being swept away.

A third reason for Peel's delay was the dangerous climate of opinion which both Anti-Corn Law League and Chartist agitation provoked in the early 1840s. Much League propaganda, with its virulent attacks on the landowners, spoke the language of class war. The League's leader, Richard Cobden, admitted as much later: 'I am afraid that most of us entered upon this struggle with the belief that we had some direct class interest in the question'. In the words of the historian W. O. Aydelotte, 'The Corn Laws question provided a focus for a great deal of pent-up resentment against the old order of things, against the aristocratic domination of the country'. This was particularly apparent during the years 1843–5 when League fortunes were beginning to wane but when it took its campaign into the agricultural areas and tried to set tenant farmer against landowner. The League spawned a Protectionist 'Anti-League' which was particularly effective in the south and east, the heartland of arable England. Peel saw the danger that commercial property would be set against agricultural property in a conflict from which only democratic causes would profit.

Peel had two overriding objectives in politics. The first was to rally and unify diverse propertied interests to stabilize and support society at a time of potentially disastrous social change; the second was to provide conditions which would stimulate economic growth and prosperity sufficient to increase living standards for the population as a whole. The activities of the League, in his view, disastrously threatened the former objective and contributed little to the achievement of the latter. In consequence, he frequently attacked the League, not primarily to gain favour with his Protectionist supporters – by 1845 such considerations hardly weighed with him at all – but because he feared the wider implications of its message. Peel clandestinely supported the specific objective for which the League was founded, but he was bitterly opposed to the wider, anti-aristocratic, agenda which many League representatives espoused.

There were cogent reasons, therefore, for not repealing the Corn Laws when such action could be interpreted as giving in to powerful, class-dominated pressure. By 1845, however, important short-term economic factors were beginning to buttress Peel's intellectual conviction in favour of free trade. After a long post-war period in which corn surpluses were the norm in most of Europe's leading arable countries, and thus when the Corn Laws did in fact operate to keep domestic prices up, the mid-1840s saw widespread shortage. As events were to prove for a generation after the Corn Laws were repealed, there was no glut of European supplies waiting to flood the British market as soon as protection was removed. British landowners and farmers would not be crushed by a foreign wheat mountain because, by 1846, no such mountain existed. As Susan Fairlie puts it, 'A situation in which the Corn Laws protected the British farmer against continental post-war glut was giving way to one in which their retention threatened Britain with famine'. Looked at from Peel's point of view, the Corn Laws needed to be repealed in 1846 in the national interest. It was an additional, and by no means unimportant, benefit that the landowning classes were unlikely to suffer.

Not surprisingly, the Protectionists failed to see matters this way. As Peel knew, he could not repeal the Corn Laws without breaking up the Conservative party. Since the Protectionists found an articulate champion in Disraeli, whose debating *forte* was political and personal and who was not anyway from the landed classes, the case against repeal has tended to be seen in unduly narrow terms. It is too easy to caricature those who opposed Peel in parliament in 1846 as self-serving reactionaries defending an outmoded interest and generally standing in the way of progress. Our knowledge of how Britain developed after 1846 may lend support to that interpretation. Britain did become an overwhelmingly urban society and the power and influence of the landed interest did wane. However, contemporaries should not be condemned for their lack of knowledge of what lay in the future and, as economic historians are now agreed, the extent to which Britain had been industrialized by the middle of the 1840s has been exaggerated. The cotton trade, from which so much of the Anti-Corn Law League drew its strength, despite its enormous contribution to British exports, could still be considered just as narrow and specific an economic interest as arable farming and Manchester was certainly not in the 1840s a more 'typical' British city than Norwich or Salisbury.

The Protectionists' economic case was weak but it was not contemptible and it deserves a hearing. It rested on the undeniable fact that corn prices before the 1840s were substantially lower than they had been during the French Wars, despite protection. The average price of an imperial quarter of wheat in the 1810s had been 91s 5d (£4.57); by the 1840s it had slumped to 55s 11d (£2.80). In such circumstances, it was easy to contest the central plank of the Anti-Corn Law League's economic argument. This was that protection produced such high prices that people were forced to spend too much of their income on food, thus threatening both the expansion and the international competitiveness of industry and commerce.

Furthermore, arable farming was not prosperous enough to generate substantial profits which could be invested in those 'improvements' such as drainage and fertilizers which political economists were constantly exhorting. Many farmers, it was asserted, were moving over to pastoral rather than arable farming, since prices were more secure. This was distorting the British food market and making consumers dangerously dependent on volatile foreign supplies. Protection was needed to ensure stability of supply to the home market. Landowners could with some plausibility argue that they were under substantial pressure and hardly the unworthily privileged class tyrants of Anti-Corn Law League imaginings.

The basic weakness of this reasoning, however, was that it assumed monolithic arable depression. In reality, the Protectionist case applied with greatest force to smaller landowners and to tenant farmers. They were the most ardent defenders of Protection. Larger landowners with more resources and, probably, opportunities for diversification could ride out even lengthy periods of depression and have capital available for investment. Peel's case to the landowners made much of the new opportunities which free trade would offer to efficient farmers and his repeal proposals included both a three-year phasing out of Protection and a loan scheme to aid drainage of wet, but potentially extremely fertile, lands. From this, those with capital were best placed to benefit. The repeal of the Corn Laws did indeed stimulate agricultural efficiency and it was followed by a long period of prosperity. These years of 'High Farming', lasting roughly from 1850 to the early 1870s, seemed to vindicate Peel's optimism. It did not, however, substantially reduce the pressure on smaller or more marginal farmers. On Peel's interpretation of the iron law of economics, of course, this did not matter. Free trade would shake out the inefficient and redeploy them more productively.

Peel's announcement to his Cabinet at the end of 1845 that he intended to propose Corn Law repeal to Parliament was initially met with consternation. Eventually, however, only Viscount Stanley (who, as the Earl of Derby, would lead the post-repeal Conservatives for twenty years) and the Duke of Buccleuch pushed their reservations to resignation. The loss of two such stalwart members both of the Cabinet and of the landed interest was considered by Peel to be sufficient grounds for resignation. He knew that Lord John Russell, the leader of the Whig–Liberals, had recently publicly announced his conversion to repeal and his calculation was that, if he allowed the Whigs to pass the measure, albeit with a substantial minority of Conservatives supporting it, he might just keep his own party together.

For a few days in early December, Russell attempted to form a government. He did so without enthusiasm, however, because he knew that repeal would provoke damaging disagreements within his own party and also because of difficulties presented by potential senior ministers, especially the new Earl Grey who would not tolerate the controversial Lord Palmerston as Foreign Secretary. In the week before Christmas, Russell informed the Queen that he could not form an administration. He passed what he appropriately described as the 'poisoned chalice' of Corn Law repeal back to Peel. Peel gallantly, and as he knew fatefully, informed Cabinet members who assumed that they were about to relinquish the seals of office that: 'I am going to the Queen. . . . I will not abandon her. Whatever may happen, I shall return from Windsor as her minister.'

The debate on Peel's Corn Law bill in the first half of 1846 was of generally high quality but predictable content. Peel occupied the high ground of national interest. After carefully rehearsing the economic arguments against continued protection, he asserted that the Corn Laws could only be maintained if the nation was prepared for class conflict. He could not charge himself with 'having taken any course inconsistent with conservative principles'. More importantly, however, he wished to convince the public that his government had been 'animated with a sincere desire to frame its legislation upon the principles of equity and justice . . . the greatest object which we or any other government can contemplate should be to elevate the social condition of that class of the people with whom we are not brought into direct relationship by the exercise of the elective franchise'.

Peel's tender, if ponderous, concern for those without votes cut no ice with either Disraeli or Lord George Bentinck who between them carried the burden of the Protectionist opposition. Bentinck launched into a vituperative condemnation of Peel's inconsistencies and lack of loyalty to party and colleagues alike, accusing him of harrying Canning literally to death in 1827, of 'base and dishonest conduct . . . inconsistent with the duty of a minister to his Sovereign' and of deserting his followers. Disraeli composed numerous variations, both witty and vulgar, on the theme of apostasy, accusing Peel of causing all 'confidence in public men' to be lost by his dissimulations and faithless dealings with his supporters. His most positive contribution was to assert that Peel had betrayed more than his party; he had bent the constitution: 'Above all, maintain the line of demarcation between parties; for it is only by maintaining the independence of party that you can maintain the integrity of public men, and the power and influence of parliament itself.' Backbenchers were not slow to weigh in. Colonel Sibthorp, for example, regretted that 'the Treasury benches [were] so infested with the noxious animals called rats'.

The Corn Laws were repealed by comfortable majorities in the Commons, but only because the Whigs voted so solidly for the bill. On third reading in May 1846 Peel's majority was 98 (for repeal 327; against 229). Only 106 of the majority votes, however, were Conservative and 222 Tories voted against. Professor Aydelotte has made a detailed study of the parliamentary divisions over the Corn Laws which demonstrates clearly that the votes were not crudely cast in terms of land *versus* commerce. The great landowners who still formed the bulk of the Whig leadership voted solidly for repeal, indicating both their feeling that repeal did not threaten them and also their concern to keep the support of business and commercial interests which were much more strongly represented on the Whig–Liberal side of the House than on the Conservative.

Those of landed background in the Conservative party outnumbered commercial and other interests by about two to one. On Corn Law repeal, however, their relationship to government was far more important than their background. 86 per cent of those who had held office under Peel supported repeal, as against only 26 per cent in the rest of the party. There could be no stronger demonstration of the extent to which Peel had cut himself off from grassroots opinion and relied upon the opinions of likeminded 'experts'.

Whatever their background, Conservative MPs seem to have been sensitive to the opinions of their constituents. Most, of course, represented county seats, 'managed' boroughs under the control of landowners, or market towns with smallish electorates and dependent on the fortunes of agriculture for their prosperity. No less than 86 per cent of Conservative MPs who sat for county or university seats voted against repeal, 63 per cent of those who sat for boroughs with electorates of less than 500 did so, and 50 per cent of those who sat for the larger boroughs. The party of small landowners voted to the end according to their Protectionist beliefs or, as an increasingly irascible Peel would have termed them, their prejudices.

Peel's government resigned not over the Corn Laws, but on an Irish coercion Bill in June 1846. That Bentinck and Disraeli could keep enough of their Protectionist followers together to vote with the Whigs against a law-and-order bill shows both the bitterness of Tory hatred against Peel and an implacable determination to force his resignation. Peel was ready enough to go. He gave a muted valedictory speech to the Commons which awkwardly mingled genuine pathos and synthetic sentiment. He regretted that his name had been 'severely censured by many who . . . deeply regret the severance of party ties'. It was a cause of no regret that 'I shall leave a name execrated by every monopolist who . . . clamours for protection because it conduces to his own individual benefit' and it was his fervent hope that he would leave 'a name sometimes remembered with expressions of good will in the abodes of those whose lot it is to labour, and to earn their daily bread by the sweat of their brow, when they shall recruit their exhausted strength with abundant and untaxed food, the sweeter because it is no longer leavened by a sense of injustice'.

He was not to resume office again, though there is nothing to suggest that he believed his departure would be permanent. He took his 'Peelites' with him though he refused to lead them as a party 'in exile'. The Conservatives were not leaderless – Derby and Disraeli would rapidly see to that, but it was difficult to see how they could fashion any kind of majority in the foreseeable future. For the remaining four years of his life Peel offered advice to his Whig successors, especially on economic matters, and he played to perfection the role of pre-eminent national statesman, uncontaminated by the messy compromises which party considerations necessitated for lesser mortals.

11

Conclusion: Reputation and evaluation, 1846–50 and beyond

Peel spent the last four years of his life as an MP who consistently disclaimed any ambition to return to office. In particular, as he told Goulburn in 1847, when asked whether there might be any basis for reuniting the Conservatives, he was 'not inclined to undertake the painful and thankless task of reconstructing a party'. He was greatly relishing the role of elder statesman which circumstances had cast him to play. He willingly appeared above the party battle, having put the nation's interests before his own career and having done so, moreover, in ways which preserved his own integrity.

It is not surprising that he remained on close personal terms after 1846 with the Queen's husband Prince Albert to whom he had acted since the Prince's arrival in England almost as a private political tutor. He confided to Albert his views about political parties. He regarded it as a matter of pride that he had made few concessions to party interests. 'However much I have been blamed for not showing more deference to a great Party . . . all I have to regret is that I shewed so much.' Peel's interest in the great questions of the day never flagged. Had he not met with his fatal riding accident in 1850, at a time when the Whig government was showing few signs of competence and stood low in public esteem, it is at least possible that he would have been tempted by an offer from the monarch to head a government based on national, rather than party, principles. Peel's survival might well have postponed the complete polarization of parties which Disraeli had advocated in 1846.

Peel used his enormous residual authority between 1846 and 1850 to support the Whig government in its continuation of the liberal economic policies he had done so much to nourish. He offered advice to the new Chancellor, Sir Charles Wood, on economic policy and the technicalities of his banking legislation; he defended the Bank Charter Act when it came under Protectionist attack during a commercial crisis in 1847; in 1848–9 he strongly supported the repeal of the Navigation Acts which remained the last significant barrier to making Britain a free trade nation. It is true that his last vote in the Commons was with the Conservatives against an aspect of foreign policy supported by the controversial foreign secretary Viscount Palmerston but he stressed that his vote had been determined by his own judgement not by party considerations. As he told his own erstwhile foreign secretary, the Earl of Aberdeen, in 1850, he stood firmly behind 'those who have had enough of party connections and are resolved to keep themselves free from its engagements'.

To the end, Peel's views on party remained paradoxical. Most of the 112 Conservatives who voted with Peel over the Corn Laws in 1846 stayed together in opposition as 'Peelites'. Sixty-nine were returned to Parliament in the 1847 general election; only ten were defeated. About thirty new 'Liberal Conservative' free traders were elected. Among the Peelites were some of Britain's ablest politicians. Two of them, Aberdeen and Gladstone, were future prime ministers. Most had been trained, directly or indirectly, in the Peelite virtues of administrative expertise and service to the nation. It is a tribute both to Peel's educative influence and also to his domination of affairs that such an elite corps of politicians remained as a separate grouping, sustaining his ideals but failing to benefit from his leadership.

In a political career not otherwise noted for generating expressions of personal warmth, Peel undoubtedly had not only the respect of his old ministerial colleagues but even their love. Henry Hardinge called him 'My great Master and generous friend' and Gladstone in 1853 referred to him glowingly as 'my great teacher and master in public affairs'. Lord Lincoln told Lady Peel the month after her husband's death: 'I never take a step in public life without reflecting on how *he* would have thought of it.'

However, Peel's ostentatiously manned vantage point above the fray after 1846 was of little help to his admiring coterie. They were left without his leadership and, while he lived, would not be

73

reabsorbed into normal political life. The Peelites had been educated not to be 'party men' and those with long careers ahead of them – most notably Gladstone – were never entirely happy playing party games or subordinating their own consciences to the dictates of prevalent party opinion. As Michael Winstanley has recently argued in the Lancaster Pamphlets series, the Liberal party under Gladstone was far from comfortable with the ideals of Gladstonian Liberalism. Gladstone remained in essence a Peelite.

From the first two days of July 1850, as sympathetic crowds gathered outside his house in Whitehall Gardens waiting for news of the mortally injured man, the tendency has been to praise Peel's achievements. Among the many memorials studied by Donald Read in his recent evaluation of Peel's reputation is the following inscription, appearing beneath a likeness of Britannia on a medal struck in his honour in 1850. 'His death was deeply deplored by men of all shades of political opinion, as the loss of a great practical statesman, earnestly devoted to the welfare of his country.'

Posterity has dealt kindly with Peel. He tends to be remembered today as the man who sacrificed his career for the good of the nation, as a gifted administrator who put national above party interests and who provided decisive and gifted leadership during a period of massive change and considerable political and social crisis. His enlightened policies are said to have given working people cheap bread, stimulated industry and laid the foundations of mid-Victorian prosperity. Peel, the wealthy landowner from an industrial background, was uniquely placed to reconcile the divergent interests of aristocracy and commerce for the benefit of the nation as a whole. It is generally held that his leadership of the Conservative party saw a necessary broadening of its base. Peel made the Conservatives a national, rather than a narrowly landed and Church-of-England, party. On this secure base, Disraeli was able to build in the late 1860s and 1870s, confirming the Conservatives as both the national and the patriotic party, an image which in the twentieth century they have most profitably maintained.

These perceptions have, in general, been supported by specialist historical opinion. Norman Gash saw Peel exercising 'unrivalled leadership at the centre of power. . . . His place as the founder of modern Conservatism is unchallengeable.' By 1850, according to Gash, 'The age of revolt was giving way to the age of stability; and of that age Peel had been the chief architect'. For Robert Blake, the election victory of 1841 was a 'striking vindication of Peel's policy'. Donald Southgate believed that Peel's 'moderation and empiricism . . . his reputation as an administrator and his supremacy as a parliamentarian' offered 'the gist of the Conservative appeal'. Donald Read concluded that Peel 'died the hero equally of the newly enfranchised, propertied middle classes, and of the unenfranchised, propertyless masses. . . . In troubled and changing times, he had satisfied the majority of the British people of all classes that the reformed political system, under strong leadership, was capable of reacting purposefully to their needs.' Finally, even the present writer, though his current position is more critical, wrote in 1983 of Peel's 'extraordinary . . . ability' and ranked his ministry of 1841–6, along with Gladstone's first, as 'the ablest of the nineteenth century'.

By now, the reader must be wondering whether this composite picture of Peel as the paragon of statesmanlike virtue is too good to be true. The reader is right to wonder! In recent years, a somewhat less flattering picture has emerged. Boyd Hilton has denied that Peel was a flexible statesman, responding rationally to each new challenge. He has argued that he was the prisoner of the economic ideology of *laissez-faire* who acted both inflexibly and dogmatically in pursuit of a predetermined policy. Ian Newbould has reappraised Peel's leadership of the Conservative party between 1832 and 1841 and concluded that he deserves much less credit for 'rebuilding' it than he has usually been given. Newbould even had the temerity to talk of 'a study in failure'. As was argued earlier (Chapter 7), the Conservative party elected in 1841 remained narrow in its support. Peel did not make the headway in the industrial areas which is usually assumed.

It is also possible to be severely critical of Peel's handling of his party. He needed Protectionist support to cement Conservative recovery in the late 1830s and, arguably, deceived both the electorate and the Protectionists about his real feelings on free trade during the 1841 election campaign. He certainly took backbench support for granted when in office. Because he despised his backbenchers' lack of experience, relevant political education and, as he saw it, absence of vision, he grossly underestimated both their case in defence of established institutions and their sense of grievance against him personally. His real feelings were revealed in a private letter to his wife written when the Protectionists failed to support him in 1845: 'How can those who spend their time hunting and shooting and eating and drinking know what were the motives of those who are responsible for the public security who have access to the best information and have no other object under heaven but to provide against danger and consult the general interests of all classes?'

Peel's conception of party may be criticized as both narrow and selfish. In the 1830s, he had seen more clearly than most the implications of 1832 for political reorganization in the constituencies. What he had not seen, or more likely had chosen to ignore, was that party was becoming a dynamic factor whose importance in government would inevitably grow. The backbench case that Peel deserved his fate in 1846 is, at the least, a reasonable one. Between 1841 and 1845 Peel either ignored his followers' sensibilities or bludgeoned them into submission. He proved himself untrue to their Tory principles on Ireland, on religion, on commerce and, finally and fatally, on the English landed interest itself.

Norman Gash seems almost as contemptuous of the Protectionist Tories as was his idol. He wrote that 'The essence of Conservatism was a government ethic and not a party interest . . . the party broke up in 1846 because the majority forsook the ethic for an interest'. Gash, however, seems to be confusing Conservatism with Peelism and asserting that all the nobler aspects of the former were attributes of the latter. It might be more accurate to conclude that the success of Peelism, as Peel himself came to recognize, depended on support from men whose political views had become diametrically opposed to his own. He had courted them in the 1830s; their education in the need to accept 'modest reform' he had begun. Once safely in office in 1841, however, he took their continued support for granted and adopted policies which offended their every sensibility.

It is not necessary to accept the Protectionists' views or to deny the intellectual superiority of the Peelites to conclude that Peel's government betrayed a party trust. In pursuing his own vision of the national interest in the 1840s, Peel neglected his power base. By 1846, the essence of Conservatism had to be a fusion of government ethic with party interest. Peel fell, his party broke up and was forced to endure a generation in the political wilderness, because Peel tried to subordinate party to both an ethic and an ideology entirely foreign to it.

In essence, Peel was an expert who devoted his political career to developing professional expertise in government and administration. The benefits of this are clear. He got things done. His legislative record is second to none in nineteenth-century politics. He dominated the House of Commons not by natural oratory and certainly not by flattery. He just knew more about the subject under discussion than almost anyone else in the House. He invariably mastered his brief. The negative aspects of 'expertism', however, are worth stressing. They include intolerance, aloofness and arrogance. Peel was persistently criticised for all three vices during a long career which was far more viciously controversial for much of its span that the fulsome tributes of 1850 might suggest. He was also surprisingly sensitive to criticism and too readily looked for personal, rather than political or intellectual, reasons to explain it.

Like many experts, also, Peel lacked political sensitivity. He believed that those who knew should rule and that those who did not had a duty to defer to the opinions of their professional and intellectual betters. Among those who 'did not know' he readily consigned to the outer limits of his condescension perhaps three-quarters of the House of Commons. For a politician, he relied on a dangerously narrow circle of intimates. In Walter Bagehot's words, written in 1856, he 'was a reserved, occupied man of business'. He did not take kindly to being interrupted. He probably worked too hard and there is plenty of evidence that his judgement during the Corn Law crisis was warped not only by purblind self-belief and contempt for the arguments of his opponents but also by exhaustion.

Let us look further into Bagehot's perceptive, but little-remembered, assessment of Peel. Bagehot is best known for his superb dissection of the British constitution in the middle years of the nineteenth century. He was also, however, a shrewd and practised observer of political affairs. He urged his readers to remember not only 'the great legislative acts which we owe to his trained capacity, every detail of which bears the impress of his practised hand'. They should also recall his earlier career: 'his name was once the power of the Protestant interest, the shibboleth by which squires and rectors distinguished those whom they loved from those whom they hated'. He never escaped the consequences of that earlier career and, in the end, they brought him down.

Bagehot provides a further important insight. Peel has been widely praised for his innovations. In reality, he was happier to systematize and codify than to innovate. He possessed administrative gifts of a high order; he was not a creator. As Bagehot put it, 'He could hardly have created anything. His intellect, admirable in administrative routine, endlessly fertile in suggestions of detail, was not of a class which creates . . . a new idea.' In a more profound sense, too, Peel was happier looking back. Most of his reforms were concerned with making old institutions work better, thus preserving their life. He preferred to see himself as the servant of the Crown. Perhaps it was his lack of imagination which prevented his appreciating what was so clear to Disraeli: party had become the central element in political life in early Victorian Britain. Peel certainly possessed the self-confidence and political will to push ahead once he was convinced that he had chosen the right course. Party considerations were of relatively little consequence to him. Given his character and administrative training, it is not really a paradox that Peel became the natural conservative who broke up the Conservative party.

Select bibliography

This is intended to be an aid for teachers and students to interesting and important work on Peel and his times. It is arranged by category and is highly selective.

Useful recent textbooks and general interpretations

N. Gash, *Aristocracy and People, 1815–65* (London: Arnold, 1979) and E. J. Evans, *The Forging of the Modern State, 1783–1870* (London: Longman, 1983) have now established themselves as texts which students have found valuable. To these might be added two recent books in the Longman *Seminar Studies* series dealing, respectively, with the earlier and later parts of Peel's career. These are E. J. Evans, *Britain before the Reform Act: Politics and Society, 1815–32* (1989) and P. Adelman, *Peel and the Conservative Party, 1830–50* (1989). See also the useful brief summary of the crowded politics of the 1830s and 1840s by R. Stewart, *Party and Politics, 1830–52* (London: Macmillan, 1989).

Biographies

Peel has not attracted as many biographical studies as some other major political figures. The quality of those most accessible to students is, however, very high and can be safely recommended. Much the most authoritative study is that by Norman Gash first published in 1961 but recently reissued in a two-volume format: *Mr. Secretary Peel* (London: Longman, 1985) takes the story to 1830 and *Sir Robert Peel* (London: Longman, 1986) completes the biography. As might be expected, Gash, though not uncritical, takes a much more favourable view of his subject than some more recent specialist studies do. D. Read, *Peel and the Victorians* (Oxford: Blackwell, 1987) is a splendid attempt to explain Peel's reputation and his hold over the Victorian imagination.

Studies of politics in the time of Peel

(a) BOOKS

The two earlier Lancaster pamphlets by the present author, *The Great Reform Act of 1832* (1983) and *Political Parties in Britain, 1783–1867* (1985) are, it is hoped, useful and succinct introductions to the sometimes tricky and definitionally awkward issue of party and party government. Many more detailed studies exist, reflecting a recent explosion of interest in the subject. Two much older studies, however, may still be consulted with profit: N. Gash, *Politics in the Age of Peel* (London: Longman, 1983) and G. Kitson Clark, *Peel and the Conservative Party* (2nd edn, London: Cass, 1964). N. Gash, *Reaction and Reconstruction in English Politics, 1830–52* (Oxford: Oxford University Press, 1965) was a major reinterpretation which still has much to offer. Peel's involvement in the economic debates of the period 1815–30 forms a small part of Boyd Hilton's *Corn, Cash, Commerce: The Economic Policies of the Tory Governments of 1815–30* (Oxford: Oxford University Press, 1977).

The best overall study of developments and tribulations in the Conservative party in the 1830s and 1840s is probably R. Stewart, *The Foundation of the Conservative Party, 1830–67* (London: Longman, 1978). D. Southgate (ed.), *The Conservative Leadership, 1832–1932* (London: Macmillan, 1974) includes an article by Gash on the leadership of Wellington and Peel. See also Robert Blake, *The Conservative Party from Peel to Thatcher* (London: Fontana, 1985).

Some more specialist works on politics and political attitudes have recently been published. I. Newbould, *Whiggery and Reform, 1830–41* (London: Macmillan, 1990) performs the extremely valuable, and long overdue, task of reinterpreting the 1830s from a Whig perspective, rather than through the Peelite prism. P. Mandler, *Aristocratic*

Government in the Age of Reform (Oxford: Oxford University Press, 1990) performs a similar service but in the context of explaining the resilience of aristocratic ideals in politics. Its focus, too, is primarily Whig/Liberal. R. Brent, *Liberal Anglican Politics: Whiggery, Religion and Reform, 1830–41* (Oxford: Oxford University Press, 1987) examines the religious issue which was of such importance in stimulating Conservative revival in the 1830s.

The Protectionists have been studied much more seriously in the past generation. No longer can they be safely reduced to the status of 'idiot-reactionaries' entirely fitted for the contumely of Sir Robert. For this necessary service, scholars are primarily indebted to the work of R. Stewart, *The Politics of Protection: Lord Derby and the Protectionists, 1841–52* (Cambridge: Cambridge University Press, 1971) and T. I. Crosby, *English Farmers and the Politics of Protection, 1815–52* (Brighton: Harvester, 1977).

In addition to the studies above, a study of the Peel government of 1841–6 is provided in T. I. Crosby, *Sir Robert Peel's Administration* (Newton Abbot: David and Charles, 1976). On the Anti-Corn Law League, see N. McCord, *The Anti-Corn Law League* (2nd edn, London: Unwin, 1968) and D. A. Hamer, *The Politics of Electoral Pressure* (Hassocks: Harvester, 1977), ch. 5.

(b) ARTICLES

A venerable article by Norman Gash, 'Peel and the Party System, 1830–50' *Transactions of the Royal Historical Society* 5th series I (1951), pp. 47–59 remains useful. Two much more recent ones by him concentrate on the growth of party: 'The Organization of the Conservative Party, 1832–46', *Parliamentary History* I (1982), pp. 137–59 and II (1983), pp. 131–52. The other articles cited here take issue with some of Gash's judgements. Boyd Hilton, 'Peel: A Reappraisal', *Historical Journal* XXII (1979), pp. 585–614 argues that Peel was imprisoned in *laissez-faire* ideology to the detriment of his wider political judgement. Ian Newbould has tried to set Peel's party political achievement in a wider, and more sceptical, context in 'Sir Robert Peel and Conservative Party, 1832–41: A Study in Failure?', *English Historical Review* IIC (1983), pp. 529–57 and 'Whiggery and the Growth of Party, 1830–41', *Parliamentary History* IV (1985), pp. 137–56. Angus Hawkins, '"Parliamentary Government" and Victorian Political Parties, c. 1830–80', *English Historical Review* CIV (1989), pp. 639–69 is also valuable in providing a wider context.

On the operation of the Corn Laws, Susan Fairlie, 'The Nineteenth-Century Corn Law Reconsidered', *Economic History Review* 2nd series XVIII (1965), pp. 562–75 remains extremely useful. The electoral implications have been investigated by G. Kitson Clark, 'The Electorate and the Repeal of the Corn Laws', *Transactions of the Royal Historical Society* 5th series I (1951), pp. 109–26.

Primary Sources

Both undergraduates and sixth-formers are now encouraged to make use of primary sources in certain aspects of their work. It is not possible to provide a full indication of the voluminous published primary sources on Peel and the politics of his age. However, three sources may be useful as a starting point. *The Memoirs of Sir Robert Peel* (2 vols, London, 1857) contain much useful material, including the full text of the Tamworth Manifesto and Peel's own careful and detailed explanation of his decision to repeal the Corn Laws. G. C. Greville, *Journals of the Reigns of George IV and William IV* (3 vols, London, 1874) are a political insider's skilfully crafted, and frequently indiscreet, memoirs of the times in which he lived. They are lively and they offer a non-Tory appraisal of Peel. Both of the above are available in many research libraries, such as those in Universities and in large city centres. Material on Peel can be found more accessibly in M. R. D. Foot and H. C. G. Mathew (eds), *The Gladstone Diaries* (Oxford: Oxford University Press). Vol. 3, published in 1974, includes material from the 1841–6 ministry which gave William Gladstone his first experience of political office. Representative, but necessarily brief, documentary selections are, of course, also accessibly provided in the two Seminar Studies by Evans and Adelman quoted above, and these might perhaps act as a starting point.